Contents

THE CHURCH ON THE HILL

The Church on the Hill

The Remarkable Rebirth of a Local Church

MICHAEL BUNKER

MARC
The British Church Growth Association

Front cover design by John Herbert

British Library Cataloguing in Publication Data

Bunker, Michael
    The church on the hill.
    1. Great Britain. Christian church
    I. Title
    274.1'0828

    ISBN 0-86065-661-6 MARC
        0-948704-14-4 BCGA

The BCGA gratefully acknowledges the help
of the Drummond Trust

Production and Printing in Great Britain for
MARC, an imprint of Kingsway Publications,
Lottbridge Drove, Eastbourne, E. Sussex BN23 6NT by
Nuprint Ltd, Harpenden, Herts AL5 4SE

I

Early Days

At the time of the terrible riots in Tottenham on 6th October 1985, I had been Vicar of St James', Muswell Hill, for seven years. Some eight months earlier I had been appointed Area Dean of West Haringey — the borough of both Tottenham and Muswell Hill. But our link with Tottenham is much closer than geographical.

On the night of 6th October, a policeman was brutally murdered. That policeman was PC Keith Blakelock. He was part of our church family — the husband of Liz, who only a few months previously had professed faith in Christ. Keith was the father of three boys who had each spent several years in our church school and been involved in church activities. Keith's funeral was planned for 11th December and I was to take the service, with the Bishop of Edmonton and our Archdeacon also taking important roles. Just a few weeks earlier these same two leading churchmen, with my fellow Area Dean in East Haringey, had taken the funeral of Mrs Jarrett — the mother whose death was seen by some as the final catalyst that sparked off these riots.

I can well remember waiting outside the main door of the church for the funeral cortège. Standing there, looking at the huge bank of reporters and photographers across the road from the church, the crowds in the street, and the men and women of the police-force lining the route, I thought: 'What am I doing here?' Everyone seemed to be confident that I was in charge. The church was absolutely packed to the doors with about 800 mourners: Liz Blakelock and her family, relatives and friends; people from our church family; row upon row of uniformed colleagues of Keith's; and many from our Muswell Hill community who had come to mourn their Beat Officer's tragic death, and to support Liz and her family in their grief. All these people, including the Mayor, the Home Secretary and the Commissioner of Police, were waiting for me to begin the service. My thought then, as it has often been during my time as Vicar here at St James' was—'Amazing Grace'.

I was uneasy with the cameras, yet I was confident that all would be well: that the service would flow reverently, that many would find support and comfort from it, and that I would be able to cope. This confidence was not *self*-confidence—I had learned many years earlier not to bank on self-reliance too much. Although I believe that people are 'wonderfully made' with great potential and dignity, I have come to realise that we cannot place too much weight on our human ability. The very fact that I was standing there as a minister of the Gospel was due entirely and supremely to God's amazing grace.

Surrounded by that great crowd of people I reflected that I had now been a Christian for some twenty-five years or more. Before God invaded my life I wasn't particularly anti-Christian, just indifferent.

As a young man I had thought that Christianity didn't really apply to me at all. Most of my childhood and teenage years were spent in Gainsborough, North Lincolnshire. The first home I can remember was a very simple terraced 'cottage', now demolished. This housed my mother, my brother Dick, and my sister Judy, and later my father when he came back from India after the Second World War. We didn't have a bathroom, so we were sent off to the public baths for that luxury. We shared our lavatory with our neighbours. As a boy I hated this especially. It always seemed so dark (there was no electric light) and cold, and it housed a great array of spiders.

My parents sent me to the local church primary school which I enjoyed. I loved 'games' but I don't recollect working at anything else. I assumed that knowledge could be absorbed through the pores, and as my education was interrupted by having to follow my father around England while he was in the Army, until he went to India, this attitude didn't help greatly.

The church itself never really made an impact on me at this time, though I did learn Bible stories there. But God drew upon this accumulation of biblical awareness and background knowledge in my conversion to Christianity. I remember having to pump the organ at the church to which the school was attached. It was my first opportunity to influence the church! The organist sat there on his organ stool, while I was tucked round the corner out of sight, pumping the long handle that filled the diaphragm full of air. There was a lead weight on a piece of string which indicated how full or empty the diaphragm was. I remember being greatly tempted to slip quietly out of the back door and leave the organ to die gradually. Only fear of the consequences prevented me.

I can't recall doing anything outstanding while at school, though I do remember being made captain of school and making a totally disastrous speech. I vividly remember being told I had failed the eleven-plus examination. I was greatly affected by that failure, although it wasn't to be my last! I ran home deeply upset, though not showing it—after all I was school captain. I was determined from then onwards not to be a loser, even if I felt I was.

My next school was the one for all the eleven-plus failures—the local secondary modern. I dreaded it. It appeared to me to be full of the town's roughs and toughs. However, I made some good friends and enjoyed my time there.

In those days it wasn't possible to take 'O'Levels at a secondary modern school, so at fifteen years of age, without any qualifications to my name, I left. I don't remember anything about the Christian content of the syllabus that was taught, although I was impressed by the personal encouragement of some of the teachers. By the end of my time there I had become captain of the football, cricket and swimming teams, and was Headboy. I greatly admired the Headmaster. He was tall, upright and very gentle, but also firm.

Throughout my teenage years I have no recollection of anyone saying anything to me about Christ, and the need to be committed to him, but mercifully I never fell foul of any great social evil. I was keen on most sports and soon took up rowing on the River Trent which skirted the town. This introduced me to drinking the 'odd jar' with the older members at the club's 'local', but thankfully it never got out of hand.

After leaving school I spent a year at the local technical college before joining my father and older brother at Marshall's—one of the two major engineering works in the town. I greatly enjoyed my five-year apprenticeship there, especially the dayrelease scheme that eventually enabled me to gain my very first qualification.

My contact with the Christian church was now remote. Very occasionally I went with some friends to the town's parish church. This wasn't because of a deep searching for God. It was just something to do, and some of our girlfriends also went there. It seemed very dull and empty as I recall. There was a good choir and an impressive organ but only a small congregation.

A group of us from the rowing club went on a skiing holiday to Austria. This holiday was a turning point in my life, for there I met Mary who was later to become my wife, she was staying with a group of nurses at a neighbouring hotel in the same village. It was Mary who would be God's agent in leading me to Christ.

After the holiday we continued to keep in touch, first by letter and then by more and more frequent trips to London. Mary was a student nurse at the Middlesex Hospital at the time. I had lots of friends, but she was different. I wanted to be with her all the time. When I wasn't, I spent the time thinking how and when I could arrange yet another trip to London!

As the months went by I realised I couldn't keep this up, not least because of the catastrophic impact these excursions to London were having on my personal finances. It certainly wasn't helping my career prospects either. I was always tired, having rushed to catch the train on Friday, spent a whirlwind of a weekend in London, and travelled back on the last possible train on Sunday night.

Being the sort of person who sees difficulties as obstacles to be overcome rather than impossible barriers, I began to put out feelers as to the possibility of transferring my apprenticeship to London. Through the influence of one of Mary's relatives I transferred to Napiers, a large engineering firm in Acton.

On finishing my apprenticeship I was moved into the then new area of 'work study'. I was on the final lap of the Higher National Certificate in Production Engineering. I greatly enjoyed moving in management circles, investigating and analysing what others were doing and helping them to be more effective in their work—a concern that has stayed with me ever since.

By now my life had changed dramatically. Mary and I had married and were living in Ealing. This proved a most significant move as the vicar of our local parish church was to have a profound influence upon us. He was a godly man with a great concern to lead people to Christ.

Our spiritual development began to move at a rapid pace, although initially I wasn't that involved. One eventful evening Mary was very late back from the Middlesex Hospital where she was still working. I began to get anxious, imagining all kinds of reasons for her lateness, but never guessing the real one.

When Mary eventually arrived home I learned that on the way back from work she had been overwhelmed by the need to discover whether or not God was a reality. Unknown to me, this quest had been in the background of her life for many years. Instead of coming straight home she rang the Vicar of St Mary's, Ealing, and he invited her to call to see him. Mary raised her doubts about God. George Perman, the

Vicar, listened patiently and finally gave her a copy of *Basic Christianity* by John Stott. He also suggested that she read St John's Gospel. This she did, and eventually she was convinced not only of the reality of God, but also that God in Jesus Christ was actually seeking her. She became a Christian.

Our home was never the same again. At first I thought I was in for trouble—I hadn't bargained for a religious wife! While there were some activities I tolerated smilingly, such as Mary's Bible reading and praying, I found others more difficult to cope with. I was happy to go with her to church on Sunday. Not that it meant much to me. What it did mean, however, was that I would get a chance to talk to a couple of other newly-weds whom we had got to know through the church—John and Kath Bausor. The Vicar of St Mary's had introduced them to us soon after our initial contact with the church. I had never met people like them before. I had the impression they would do anything for us and that nothing was too much trouble.

Mary constantly quizzed me about my spiritual progress. For some time all her questions were like a foreign language to me. Wonderfully however, while I was under some pressure to consider these matters in a way I had not done before, I never resented it. Secretly I had to admit that this change in Mary had fringe benefits for me. She was certainly different, but I was never the loser. What she did was never at my expense. In fact, I always seemed to be the centre of her concern. I was very happily married. Life was better than I ever dared imagine. Mary seemed so relieved to know she had a Saviour in Christ, but I had no such concern. I knew I wasn't perfect, for I was aware that I had wronged a number of people, but I didn't fully understand what she meant by 'sin'.

Time passed by, but almost every evening I would be questioned about my spiritual progress. Had I thought about Christ? Didn't I realise I needed a Saviour? And so the questions and challenges continued. I mentally ducked and weaved like a scrum half, and with some success. But while Mary couldn't have been more direct in her questions, I never once felt rejected for saying, 'I'm not sure.' In fact, what set me thinking more than anything was the personal change that had taken place in Mary. I couldn't ignore it, though I might try to explain it away. It affected me at a very deep level.

I didn't quite understand what it was that I had to do, but 'doing something' was obviously important, so I decided to take a deeper interest in spiritual matters—in Christianity. But as I tried to be 'more Christian', so I discovered a growing sense of failure and guilt. I felt as if I was living two lives. At home I was basically 'Christian', but at work I was my old self, one of the boys. These two lives were quite different from one another and soon caused an inner tension which began to tell on my happy home and work.

Many people drift into faith and cannot be very specific about the time when they first became committed to Christ. But others, like me, can remember the moment as if it happened only yesterday. It began like most days during that period, with me trying to behave as a Christian at work, as Mary did at home, but with little success and a growing sense of weakness and powerlessness. These feelings were new and very irritating to me. I was very unsettled. I wanted peace, but couldn't find it. I'm not sure how long this unsettled state went on for, but I very clearly remember the climax of it all.

I usually travelled home from work by tube to Ealing Common station and then walked across the common itself to our home in Disraeli Road backing onto the famous Ealing Studios. As I walked, a verse from John's Gospel came to mind—Mary had quoted it to me often enough—'As many as received him, to them gave he power to become the sons of God' (Jn 1:12, Authorised Version).

I knew that receiving Christ meant trusting him as my Saviour. While trying to make up my mind what to do, I sifted not only what I had recently been told by Mary and had heard on the Sundays I had gone with her to church, but also a whole collection of information from the religious background of my childhood. What I had never done before and was being challenged to do now was to ask, 'What do the stories about Christ add up to?' Previously I had considered the Gospels merely as religious stories. Now I was having to view them in a different light. This same material was presented to me as truth about someone who could, it was said, assist me with my problem, my conflict. This Jesus of the Gospels was relevant to my present plight and I should seriously consider asking him for help.

Until my walk across Ealing Common I had never considered this Jesus of the New Testament to be at all relevant to my life. But now I was rethinking my assessment of him. It wasn't that the academic arguments had won me over. It wasn't that I had some deep mystical experience. This changed attitude towards Christ sprang from an acute sense of need, and because some people around me, who had greatly impressed me, said that he was relevant to them. These people, though clearly very religious (they went to church twice on Sunday and said grace before all meals!) were actually down to earth and very interesting. What impressed me even more at the time was that they seemed to be interested in me and valued my friendship, for we were often invited to their homes.

I hated living two lives—one at home and another at work. I longed to be someone with more integrity than I felt I had. I would ask myself the question, what would Mary make of me if she really knew how I behaved at work during the day? Would she even recognise me? Similarly, if my inner thoughts could have been heard by my colleagues at work, what would they think? I often felt trapped into saying things and behaving in a way I wasn't comfortable about. The usual topic of conversation at work wasn't of the highest to say the least. Thoughts and questions like these flashed across my mind at this time. It was a period when I weighed my attitude to life—assessed its quality, or rather lack of it—and reviewed my thinking about Christ and his relevance to all that was happening to me.

On that evening's walk home after a day's work I did 'receive him'. I did so because I didn't know what else to do. I did so because others had told me how he had dealt with their problems. Could he deal with mine, my personal weaknesses? There were things that I wanted to do, certain moral choices that I wanted to make but found I couldn't. I had been told that the Christ who had died was alive; I knew the stories and some of the promises of help. But the challenge confronting me was, do I trust him? Was I prepared to accept his help on his terms? I cannot remember faltering for a moment about the decision I had to make. It seemed so clear cut: it was either this or go-it-alone. Strangely enough, I felt that while I was being challenged to receive Christ I was actually the one who was being received. I tried to form a prayer of commitment. I knew absolutely nothing about the inspiration and authority of Scripture. But I believed that the words of John 1:12 were true and I trusted and followed them from that moment on, believing that Christ would help me. He did, he has, and he's wonderful!

I never thought of noting the date of this walk across Ealing Common. What I do know is that from the moment I became a committed Christian my feet hardly touched the ground. Slowly but surely we were drawn into the life of the church, and in due course I was confirmed.

Mary and I had married in the summer of 1957. Between then and 29th September 1960, when I commenced theological training, a very great deal happened.

At someone's suggestion we spent a week at the Keswick Convention. It rained and rained and rained, but the ministry of the week had a most profound effect upon us both. The worship was an inspiration, but it was the teaching and preaching that really gripped me. I wanted as thorough a knowledge of Scripture as these speakers seemed to have, and I wanted to expound it as clearly as they did. Every sermon seemed as if it was being spoken first to me.

It was at the annual missionary meeting that I heard a sermon on John 2:5 which was to be another turning point in my life. God spoke to me directly through his living word in Scripture. The word that afternoon was that same word that the mother of Jesus gave to the servants at the memorable wedding to which they had been invited. They had run out of wine and Jesus' mother said to the servants, 'Do whatever he tells you.' He told them to do something which seemed to them, I'm sure, quite silly. What was wanted was wine, but he asked them to fill the containers with water. Strange as that command was, the servants did as they were told and the guests were able to enjoy wine that was 'the best of the day'.

It was through this message that God called me to full-time ministry, and thankfully Mary was also challenged. When we returned home we shared with our friends and the vicar what it was that God seemed to be calling us to. People were clearly delighted, but I noticed also some surprise. After all, we hadn't been Christians very long!

I was very excited at the thought of going to Oak Hill Theological College, but there were certain aspects of the three years ahead that I did not relish. In those days there was no such thing as married quarters. We had to live apart during term time for those three years. We found this hard, having only been married a short while. Because of the financial complications of it all, we had to sell our new maisonette in Ealing and move in with our friends, John and Kath Bausor, when they moved house to Edgware. They were a great help and support to Mary during this time, especially while I was at college.

A great many changes have taken place in theological training since my time at college. Some of them were no doubt necessary. For a while I felt all at sea with the studies, but I thoroughly enjoyed my time and benefited enormously from what was on offer. In those days there was a great emphasis on expanding the students' biblical and theological understanding and knowledge. We were expected to involve ourselves in a wide variety of the ministries that the college organised. I was especially grateful for this, for it was virtually my first taste of Christian ministry. I made many mistakes—some amusing, lots painful.

I particularly valued the biblical emphasis of my training. As far as I was concerned it was vintage stuff. New Testament exposition was mainly in the hands of Alan Stibbs, a very gifted teacher. Some time before going to Oak Hill I had read his book *God's Church* which whetted my appetite for his lectures. I was not to be disappointed. The tutor responsible for the Old Testament lectures was F D Kidner. What a duo: Stibbs and Kidner! Everything 'FDK' did seemed so polished. He was a tremendous inspiration.

The emphasis which I appreciated most was the apparent concern of the staff to equip the students as far as possible for ministry. The outlook seemed to me to be practical, but when I left, duly qualified, I hadn't had any training in church management, little in the financial aspects of church life, and certainly none on managing a staff team, let alone its selection. Very few churches at the time had small Bible study/fellowship groups, so that was another blank area in my training. However, I did leave eager to be first and foremost a faithful curate, picking up as much experience as I could on the way to becoming a faithful pastor. The servant model of church leadership was very much stressed in our training, and rightly so, for it is the model Jesus gave us in his own ministry and teaching.

After leaving college I spent three happy years with the Rev Joe Johnson at St James', Alperton, near Wembley. At that time it was a small struggling church. I was very much the vicar's assistant and was clearly directed in all I had to do. Although I found this difficult at times, I was able to knuckle down and, in fact, greatly enjoyed and appreciated my time there.

When the time drew near for leaving Alperton, Mary and I had to examine the question, what next? We hadn't yet discovered whether God wanted us in England or overseas. I wrote to all the missionary societies I could think of, outlining details about myself and the family (by now Nicolas and Hugh were very much on the scene, aged three-and-a-half and two years respectively) and sharing something of my accumulated experience as I perceived it and what I thought were my strengths and shortcomings. A few showed some interest, but OMF was keen and it seemed that the door to Malaysia might be opening up for us.

This was a challenging time. I was very excited about the prospects of working in Malaya. I had read books and spoken to experienced missionaries. The doors seemed to spring open—it looked as if we would be going. Then at the very last moment the final Candidates' Conference decided, on a number of counts, not to recommend us. I was very disappointed and thoroughly deflated for several days. But I was comforted by the trouble OMF had taken over our case. Clearly, they had done all they could to discern God's will about our future with them. Although painful, the experience was valuable for it confirmed that God did indeed want me to be a missionary, but in England and not Malaysia.

Secure in our calling we moved our home and ministry to St Helen's, Merseyside, to work with Canon Ken Coates and his team. I was to be Curate-in-charge of St Andrew's, one of the daughter churches in this large and important parish in the Liverpool diocese. We had a marvellous time, making lasting friendships. I loved every minute of my four years there.

It was a real privilege to work on a staff team at last. When I joined it included the Vicar, the Curate-in-charge of the daughter church of St Mary's, a curate who worked with the youth of the parish at the parish church, a parish worker, and a Church Army officer who ran the mission centre. Staff meetings with the vicar were always great fun. We worked hard, enjoying fulfilment and happiness. I learned a lot from Ken Coates, a man of boundless energy and good humour. A gifted preacher and organiser, I was always impressed by the care he took when leading public worship.

I well remember the first service I had to take— midweek Holy Communion at 7.30 am in the parish church. After it was all over I drove back home feeling quite pleased with myself. To my astonishment the vicar's car was already standing outside our house. I discovered him waiting for me in my study with a smile and a few notes. He made a number of warm encouraging noises and then went on to point out a few verbal mistakes I had made—'according to the book'. It was all done in good humour, but it did have the effect of putting me on my toes. Many years later, one of our morning services at St James', Muswell Hill, was televised live. Following this I had a number of phone calls and letters saying how helpful people had found the service. The one I appreciated most was a call from dear Ken Coates saying how well he thought the service went.

During our time in St Helen's the life of the church seemed to grow, although in those days we never consciously measured or studied what was happening. There was still a good tradition of church attendance, so most of the churches in the area had reasonable congregations and most Christian activities were well supported. It was therefore quite a shock for us when it seemed that I was being called to be Vicar of St Matthew's, Muswell Hill, which at that time seemed far from flourishing.

2

The Church down the Road

I viewed our move to Muswell Hill with mixed feelings. I knew I would miss the support and fun of being part of a staff team. St Matthew's had very few lay leaders and I was to be 'the staff team'—the one and only full-time member of staff—for some considerable time. St Matthew's had a small and largely elderly congregation, very different from the one I had been part of for the four years previously. I was leaving a major parish ministry in the Liverpool diocese to go to a depressed, declining and obscure little church. But I was to be their vicar and that excited me—and I was convinced it was what God wanted me to do.

It wasn't what I had dreamed of during my curacy days—quite the opposite. I thought that I would be at my best in parish ministry, and I hoped to become vicar of a parish church in a small town—a town large enough for me to consider it a 'large task', but not too large that it swamped me. St Matthew's had a small parish and a very small congregation, but in those early days I had high hopes. I could see that the church had potential, though at the time it had very few people who could take on leadership roles. Its style of ministry hadn't really caught up with the contemporary scene. Although the church building was sound, it was most uninspiring architecturally and very much off the beaten track. The only bus route was on the boundary of the parish. There were only three shops, and no pub or other centre of community activity in the parish. For years the church had been surrounded by a high hedge of privet and hawthorn. After a while we cut this down. I did get some help, but it was mainly a single-handed effort with a hired chain-saw. One day, when I had almost completed the task, a gentleman passed by and stopped for a chat. Apparently he had lived on the estate just down the road from the church for several years, but this was the first time he had noticed that there *was* a church behind the bushes!

The other facilities were in a far worse state of repair. The church hall needed a great deal of work done to it. It constantly looked as if it had been left to the vandals and I was forever reglazing the windows. I once glazed thirty in one week. We had another small hut which the Scouts and Cubs used. This was a wooden 'historic building' so it seemed. I was told on good authority that it was originally used as the chapel at The Great Exhibition at Wembley in 1924.

The best part of the fabric was the vicarage, built in 1957. It had a large garden surrounding it, and this, plus the church grounds, gave the impression of an almost rural setting. In addition, just behind our church there was a plot of land used as playing fields by a local school. We were greatly looking forward to living in the vicarage, but certainly felt the challenge of the task facing us.

My institution as vicar was a wonderful occasion.

Friends came from St Mary's, Ealing, and St Margarets, Edgware, where we had been based while I was at Oak Hill, as well as a coach-load from St Helen's. The Christian community of Muswell Hill also came to give their support and encouragement. The church was full—and we were full of hope. My first Sunday brought me down to earth. Both the morning and evening congregations were very small. One memorable Sunday morning my congregation consisted of the organist, a Churchwarden, my wife and one other.

What was I to do? I knew that there were a number of key areas that I had to tackle if we were to get anywhere at all. Obviously, the folk who made up the congregation were important and I tried to get to know them through visiting and various social events dreamed up to create a pleasant environment in which they could relax and I could get to know who they were and how they ticked. I also knew I had to raise their expectations and broaden their horizons, so I made a point in the first few months of preaching on the nature and function of the church. However, I soon realised that I had to be far more Christ-centred in my preaching as many of the folk didn't have a firm grasp of who Our Lord really is and what he has achieved. Mary very generously held the fort for four days while I went on retreat to replan the preaching programme. I drove to the Pembrokeshire coast and camped by the sea. During those four days I sketched out a year's sermons, virtually all from St Mark's Gospel. In this way I thought that I could concentrate on Jesus, as well as making the most of the time I had for preparation. Of couse, the congregation didn't always realise this was the case. I did 'the ministry of

Christ according to Mark', 'some parables of Jesus', 'miracles', 'the word and works of Jesus and his disciples', 'Jesus and the opposition', 'Jesus and his teaching on ...'—all subjects raised by him and referred to in St Mark's Gospel. I bought copies of St Mark's Gospel in the Good News edition for the congregation. At the same time, of course, I included themes from the Old Testament about Jesus. I'm not sure what impact all this had on the congregation, but the concentrated preparation over that year had a profound effect upon me!

I shall always be grateful to those who taught me the importance of the Scriptures for one's private life and public ministry. It was strange knowing that when I went into church and looked at the congregation with my sermon notes in front of me, I would almost certainly know everyone there by name. We very rarely had a visitor or newcomer in those days, but I often found myself preaching to those whom I hoped would be there or whom I thought should be there. It took a concentrated effort in my sermon preparation to consider who was likely to be present and to apply Scripture to them first of all. In those days I tried to discipline myself never to skimp preparation, though I was very tempted to do so on occasions. I knew I could preach for the allotted time without notes and with hardly any preparation and get away with it, but I vowed I would never preach a sermon I wasn't excited about sharing. But it was tough—for many years I never felt that people got as excited about my sermons as I did. But at least they nourished me, if no one else! Perhaps I needed more feeding than my flock at that time.

The other problem areas were finance and fabric.

The finances were not in a very healthy state, largely because the majority of the congregation were pensioners. Most of the income came from a handful of people. Although the books balanced each year and showed a surplus, there was virtually nothing for the running expenses of the ministry or improvements to the fabric, let alone outreach. Any work on the building would have to be on a do-it-yourself-and-pay-it-yourself-basis. Any major expense would have crippled us for years, so I hoped I could prop things up until the church's finances developed a sounder base. I decided, rightly or wrongly, not to call in the professionals unless I had to.

I remember going into church one Sunday and finding the boiler house flooded with about three feet of water. Everything was awash, but thankfully not the electrics. How do you remove that amount of water? I guessed there must be a way. I rang up some of the older members who informed me the church was in fact built over a stream and they had had trouble like this before, but not as bad. In the past the water had eventually subsided on its own. After looking around it was obvious that there must be an outlet somewhere. So I put on some shorts and set out to find it. This I did eventually, and slowly the water disappeared. I later discovered that there was a stream of water that flowed into the boiler through a specially prepared inlet and out through a similar outlet. I made sure both were always free flowing in the future. Just a few weeks later the boiler went out. This time the lining of the chimney had collapsed into the chamber. But I managed to get it clear and the boiler ran smoothly for a further six years.

During most weeks I spent a good many hours

trying to bring the buildings up to date. Thankfully over the years a number of practical folk did join the church and give a hand, but I became a kind of maintenance-man-cum-pastor. In the next seven years I replumbed the cold water supply to the hall, demolished the stage in the hall and built an extra room in the space, built a cupboard the full length of the hall for the playgroup that came to use the facility, mended literally hundreds of panes of glass and, later on, reordered the interior of the church. This was all achieved with a handful of people and me playing foreman! Although on reflection I have often wondered if I was right to do all this, I did earn credibility with those who came to help. I was grateful that by the time we needed more expertise than I had, we had a slightly larger congregation and some of them had a lot to contribute in this area of DIY. With this help we rewired the hall and even installed a temporary central heating system in the church. One good thing about all this was that I nearly always had something to show for my week's work.

Our main midweek activity was a central Bible study and prayer meeting which I usually led. Looking back I cannot understand why I never considered home Bible study groups, nor why I didn't see the importance of sharing the leadership of the central meeting, even though the leadership of the church did develop into a more shared activity. Indeed, I gave a major part of my energies to the area of leadership. I began to think, pray and plan how I could attract young, energetic and committed Christians to our church. I knew it was going to be difficult, for all I had to offer was a dream, a great challenge, and my friendship. It didn't seem much of a 'carrot'.

One day, out of the blue, James telephoned. He was, he informed me, a student at Oxford coming to work in London and he wanted to find a church where he could really be used. I knew just the place, I told him. James became a good friend. He worked hard with very little encouragement from the congregation. It was a long time before he was really accepted by the church membership. I felt very bad about that. He was a gracious and patient person, but he was still a student at heart and would appear on Sunday—like a lot of people do today—in a sweater, trousers and sandals. When I suggested after a while that perhaps the wardens should invite him to be a sidesman, the reply came back, 'How can we? He never comes in a suit and he never wears proper shoes'.

In spite of this kind of attitude, younger folk started to find us and to my great surprise and joy they began to stay. It wasn't automatic, however. Every visitor was warmly welcomed and either visited that week by myself or Mary, or invited back to the vicarage. We spent many hours with these newcomers. As a result of this activity I soon realised that the newcomers, often after only a few weeks of exposure to our church, had a greater vision for it than practically all the others put together.

One particularly fruitful time followed a visit to a Christian union at an Oxford University College. This resulted in a strong link with a number of students who eventually moved to London, to Muswell Hill, and to St Matthew's after they had graduated.

Then came the time when there was a complete switch round of leadership. Most of the older folk had lost heart and I suspect couldn't cope with my enthusiasm and energy. It wasn't long before we had a

PCC membership whose average age was under twenty-five. Of the churchwardens I inherited, one was already retired and the other retired two years after my arrival. My next two wardens were both in their mid-twenties — newly married, very committed, and very energetic. I had to run to keep up with them! We changed from being a largely elderly church to a student church in one leap, and this presented new problems.

One of these was the pressure on our home which I never fully realised until some years later. The problem was that we were virtually the only couple with children in the church. To make matters more complicated still, our boys are grouped in pairs. In those days we had two young teenagers, Nick and Hugh, and two younger boys, Jonathan and David. Both pairs had different needs. But the keen members in the church were eager to 'get on', and I felt I had to be with them even if the work went on into the late hours. I often came back to the vicarage to find Mary struggling with restless or sick children, worn out from their day-long demands, washing-up piled high everywhere because of the interruptions caused by the children, and callers at the door that I hadn't been able to deal with because I was elsewhere. I would then set to in the home and encourage Mary. When I look back on this period in our lives, I am profoundly thankful to God that he kept us from all the hazards that such constant activity could have brought us. It was most definitely the Lord who saw us through this period reasonably intact, for there was no one else to give us the advice and help that we needed at the time.

It is, indeed, remarkable how well our family survived. Our four boys are all young men now and a joy to us both. Although David, our youngest, is currently involved in the life of the church, the other three are not, I believe, distant from it. I know that their relationship to the Lord might be different if there had been others of their age and outlook in St Matthew's at that time, but there weren't. Their non-Christian friends had a deep influence on them, and we couldn't counter it effectively on our own. However, the boys were involved in the local Crusader group and this gave them a firm grounding in the Christian faith which we believe they will appreciate one day. I wonder how many families, like ours, owe a debt of gratitude to this fine interdenominational Christian organisation.

I am always saddened when people withdraw from active involvement in the church due to certain pressures they are undergoing. My wife Mary never did, even when we were undergoing the most profound pressures. I had to learn the hard way how to be the pastor and leader of a congregation, as well as trying to be a father and husband. We were constantly walking on a financial knife-edge as a family—a problem we found very difficult in our contemporary society. Thankfully, the boys have always enjoyed good health, but they had lots of energy and this was not always easy to channel in constructive ways.

Although Mary had to cope with a series of personal problems which fluctuated from the fairly serious to the acute, very few people, I'm sure, guessed this at the time for she never withdrew from her responsibilities. Although she never took a leadership role in the church, we did use our home a great deal. We had little choice here as the facilities in the church were very poor by contemporary standards. But I can't think of one function that had to be cancelled for reasons of Mary's health. There were times when she fell into black depression, but she never gave up or made me feel I couldn't carry on. She even went out to work to help support us during those difficult days of high inflation in the 70s.

How did she, and we, survive? I'm sure one great influence was her regular reading and meditating upon God's word. Even at her darkest moments she would sit poring over the Scriptures, finding in them support, comfort and inspiration. Her spirituality was then, as it has always been, a constant challenge to me. I have to run to keep up with her. She is the one who prevents me from turning off our allotted path. Her influence on me during this period was profound. She has always been my personal critic—which I have ultimately appreciated, though not always enjoyed—yet she listens to the word preached and that encourages me. I have always been full of bright and not-so-bright ideas. Mary has never put me down or dampened my creativity, she has helped to hone my ideas into shape for practical application.

St Matthew's grew very slowly. What growth we did enjoy was largely through young Christian graduates moving into the area and finding us. At times we had as many as sixty people at morning worship, but it very rarely rose above this, no matter how hard we tried. However, while we may not have grown much numerically, we did develop from a young group of Christians into a true church—a community with a sense of belonging coupled with a concern for mission. One reason for this was that almost every week for two years we met together as a church for lunch after our main Sunday worship.

I often pondered as to how I could help deepen the sense of community and family in the church. It was one Saturday morning, while I was preparing the vegetables for our family lunch on Sunday, that I thought, 'Why not have a church Sunday lunch?' On Saturdays Mary went to the Royal Free Hospital on nursing duty. This gave me an excuse to have time off with the boys, and we rarely had visitors or weddings on Saturday mornings. I usually helped by doing some advance preparation for our own Sunday lunch. This was no sacrifice as I've always enjoyed cooking (and eating!). The idea of cooking for a few more each Sunday didn't daunt me. I had previously organised camps, house-parties and the odd barbecue. This didn't seem that different, just more regular.

Once I'd persuaded Mary that the idea wasn't too crazy, and I'd checked that our key people would support us, the idea was launched. To my great encouragement it received enthusiastic support from the outset. Hardly a Sunday went by after this when we had fewer than thirty for lunch. We often numbered fifty or even sixty.

We did give ourselves a few Sundays off each year— one after Christmas and Easter, and the whole of August. I promised Mary that we would always have a good break every summer away from work and ministry and people. Through the generosity and help of a lot of people, this was generally achieved, though with varying degrees of success.

Incredible as it may seem, we actually enjoyed running these Sunday lunches over the next three years. For the first years it was mainly a one-man effort. To some extent it was easier that way—everything was within my control. It wasn't until later when the ministry developed that I had to start delegating jobs. I would deliver a sack of potatoes to one couple and they would deliver them peeled and ready for boiling or roasting on the Sunday morning. We also developed a 'pudding rota' leaving me with just the main course and another vegetable to prepare.

So for two years we met together first for worship, beginning at eleven o'clock, and then afterwards for lunch. Our folk would often not leave until gone three o'clock. It was during this time that we really began to get to know one another. It was too long a time to engage in superficial conversation. People began to share their joys and sorrows, their hopes and fears, their backgrounds and ambitions. The young began to get to know the elderly and vice versa. The 'trads' and the 'mods', the regular and the casual, the fringe and the flock, the committed and the nominal— through this venture we began to be a family.

At this time there was a small inner core with whom I shared most things. They were all much younger than me, but this didn't prevent them from making a sizeable contribution to the work for God at St Matthew's. This group included three couples and Paul Evans, a quiet but supportive young graduate from Oxford. Paul had landed himself a job with Price Waterhouse in the city as a trainee accountant. It wasn't long before he was our church treasurer. We started to move out of the survival mentality to one of growth and development, although on a modest scale.

The three couples had joined the church a little earlier than Paul, and all arrived on the scene at roughly the same time.

Austin and Ros Banner had been members of St Helen's, Bishopsgate, for a number of years, where the ministry of the Rev Dick Lucas had influenced them greatly. They arrived just as I was looking for two Churchwardens. I quickly pressed Austin into allowing his name to go forward for election. He was a bundle of energy and Christian enthusiasm. The person who was to become the other Churchwarden was Hugh Fisher. He and his wife, Judy had married and moved from North Finchley into a flat in our parish.

In those early years the number of hours these two young men put into the church was simply enormous. Planning meetings and small chats that developed into discussions on strategy were quite frequent, going on well into the early hours of the morning. But it wasn't all talk. These two people contributed the lion's share of help over the practical jobs too.

Hugh was an extremely efficient administrator which was a great help in many ways. As well as having a real theological sensitivity and understanding, he was a very talented DIY man, particularly in the field of electricity. With the help of a few friends he rewired the church hall, and towards the end of our time at St Matthew's he helped to install a temporary central heating system.

When it came to the move to St James', he and Judy were marvellous. Hugh took on the oversight of the children's work for several years and saw it through its most difficult period. At first it all took place in our Vicarage, which initially resembled a building site rather than a home! But Hugh soldiered on with few complaints and began to form a real team of teachers and helpers. During this time the Fishers had their first child and a good number of practical tasks to do in their own home, but they never allowed this to get in the way of their church commitments. Today the

children's work at St James' owes a great deal to this
early effort.

The other couple I must mention is Paul and Rosie
Watson. They joined us in 1973, having arrived back
from Australia where Paul, a vet, had been studying
for his PhD—on the fertility of elephants, as I
discovered to my fascination. What an interesting
guy, I thought. They quickly became key members of
the church, and Paul, who had trained as a Lay Reader
in Australia, was licensed to help me. He and Rosie
have been a great support ever since their arrival. Paul
is a very gifted pastor and after years of experience in
this role is now preparing for ordination to the
nonstipendiary ministry. Poor Rosie found my sermons
very hard going in those early days. When I discovered
his I went to see her and sympathise with her. This
was a very humbling time for me. For several weeks I
used to call round and share my thoughts for next
Sunday's sermon. Her attitude changed, as did my
sermons. Whenever there was discontent the Watsons
could be relied upon to listen, but they remained loyal
to me and supportive in many lovely and generous
ways. We have worked and worshipped together now
for some thirteen years. I have seen them develop into
people of real stature. Paul will, God willing, be a
non-stipendiary curate with me in the summer of 1988.

When the challenge eventually came for us to move
to St James', it never entered out heads to part
company. Vicar and congregation—all went together
like the people of Israel at the exodus, a family excited
by fresh opportunities and a new future.

3

The Church on the Hill

During the 1970s inflation hit the church as it hit individuals and families, especially those on fixed incomes. The clergy income was slow to keep pace with inflation, forcing many more clergy wives out of the home and the pastoral supporting role and into the role of financial supporter. If Mary had not done this I don't know how we would have survived. The Christian church owes a great debt to its ministers' wives.

Just as the clergy income was slow to move, so too was that of the church as a whole. There are now signs that Christian people are regularly increasing their giving, but sadly this has been slow to develop. The result of all this was a more critical look by the church authorities at the cost of keeping churches open and in business. This review included the manpower situation and allocation of the clergy. Deaneries were asked to examine which churches should remain, which should be closed, and which should be grouped together. I also began to examine the viability of our church and ministry.

In many respects we were not under threat as some were because of their actual situation. We had a reasonable congregation, our income had managed to rise to keep abreast of increasing costs, and our membership was younger than most and had potential. However, after some thought I came to the conclusion, largely for strategic reasons, that we should consider volunteering a merger with another church. Naturally I kept these thoughts to myself for some time. I didn't wish to be alarmist—we appeared to have a great deal going for us, and our folk really valued being part of the church family.

Eventually I drafted a report for Bill Westwood, the Bishop of the Edmonton Area, and I asked a group of our key people to consider its implications. This resulted in a reworked report with recommendations signed by my two Churchwardens, the treasurer and my Lay Reader. It received a warm response from the Bishop. Later he discussed the report again with me, promising not to forget all the work that had gone into it. We had listed a number of options for our future—all meant moving from our buildings.

Some six months later the Vicar of St James', Muswell Hill, died in office. Bill Allam was greatly loved by the church he had served for ten years. He had been unwell for some time, though he struggled on virtually until the end. Early in 1978, the Bishop asked me to see him and we discussed the possibility of my going to St James' and taking the folk from St Matthew's with me. I was excited by the prospect, the Bishop was hopeful, but there was still the question of whether or not the 'church on the hill' would want the vicar from down the road. Their reaction was 'better the devil you know than the one you don't.' I would have preferred a more inspiring sentiment but was happy to accept it, hoping that perhaps there were other reasons behind this one.

The Bishop's role was vital in all this—it was his vision that inspired the first step. He clearly didn't want the church simply to struggle on, but to be full of life and vitality. He could so easily have made a safe move and chosen a clergyman who had a proven track-record. But he took the risk of appointing someone whom he thought could be instrumental in achieving the goal. But for 'the Bishop's move', we might well have been struggling with a very different situation from our present one. There is such a need for bishops to have the same vision and courage today.

The time-span between the possibility of the move to St James' and the actual move was about five months. During this time I pondered what it would be like if I was given the chance of such a ministry. Secretly, for I couldn't share the truth with anyone, I longed for this widening of my ministry in Muswell Hill. There is, my wife tells me, a little of Walter Mitty in me. This spirit certainly had a field day during my dreaming moments. At that time St James' was struggling to keep its head above water, but it had known better days. I had a vision of it being a major church in the London Diocese once again and an important Christian centre in North London while still being a true parish church.

I knew that if such an amalgamation did get the go-ahead then I would not have the option simply to keep the status quo. We had to change or decay, as the Bishop was later to tell us. The initiative clearly lay with me to introduce and implement changes that would in due course set the church on a path to new life and vigour. If I didn't come up with some ideas and the courage to implement them there would be a great deal of disappointment and even dissatisfaction from which the church might never recover. The first six months' activities would be critical in welding the two congregations together into a unified and out-ward-looking Christian community. So, long before the task became mine I set about thinking what kind of a church St James' ought to be, bearing in mind its strategic geographical position and the make-up of the community of the parish and neighbourhood. In hind-sight I am very glad I did so, for once things started moving they did so very rapidly indeed.

What did God really expect of his church? This was the critical question which formed the hub of my thinking. For some years I had taken a special interest in all that had been written about the nature and function of the church. Many Christians had helped to clear the fog in my own mind and guide my thinking over how to turn theory into practice. From my reading and study of Scripture, the church's task seems to be threefold. Our first priority is towards God: we owe him our worship, gratitude and obedience. Secondly, we have a clear duty to the world at large. As his privileged and redeemed people we should reflect to others the excellence of the Saviour who has so richly blessed us as individuals and a Christian community. Our third duty lies in yet another direction: towards each other. We are a family, and as such we have a responsibility to help, encourage, exhort and forgive one another.

How was I to educate and encourage St James' congregation, which was largely thinking about its own survival, to think more about God and the world in which it was placed, as well as to develop a proper and healthy regard for one another? How was I to help build a church which would have a substantial ministry among its individual members, so as to move away from the idea that the clergy could and should do most of the ministering? How would I instigate such a radical rethink? The answer was clearly with difficulty, and only with God's help, for I was, and still am, merely a parish pastor with only an average amount of ability and expertise.

Added to these questions was the further one of how to amalgamate two different congregations into one family without sacrificing the vision just outlined. I knew that one of my first priorities would be to get to know the people of St James' as quickly as possible. My predecessor had been greatly loved and much respected, and they still mourned his loss. I knew I had to seek, somehow, to fill the gap as best I could. This would mean giving these people the first call on my time and distancing myself from the St Matthew's folk, without neglecting them, for at least a year. The way they coped with this and their appreciation of my position is to their great credit.

In all this I felt quite isolated, for I was unable to share my hopes, desires and thoughts with many people. I certainly couldn't discuss them with the St Matthew's folk, close to me as they were, because of the sacrifices I would have to ask them to make. The close family relationships we shared would probably have to give way to something more structured and formal as I made it a priority to get to know the people of St James'.

Neither could I find help and support from the folk at St James', for they too would have to make sacrifices. At this time St James' was conservative and cautious in worship and style of ministry. Its life had changed very little for years. Now, suddenly it would be adopting a whole congregation from another church. It couldn't expect to remain the same. The people of St Matthew's would be giving up their independence and individuality and it wouldn't be right for St James' not to make changes in order to help them adjust to this new situation. I knew I would have to think carefully about these changes and lead the people into them and through them. I feared this would be difficult—and I wasn't wrong.

I was extremely fortunate at this time in having a couple of close friends who had lived in Muswell Hill for a number of years, yet who were members neither of St James' nor St Matthew's. Brian and Rachel Griffiths lived very close to St James' church and their children were being educated at St James' School, as ours were, but they were members of a neighbouring church in Highgate.

I first met Brian through Muswell Hill Crusaders as their children were members when we moved into the district. Being discreet and mature Christians, I was able to share my hopes and ideas with them over the next six months or so. These ideas were chiselled and shaped through hours of discussion. Rachel was particularly patient, for I fear I overstepped the mark from time to time and kept them up talking far too long. These were, however, very formative days and I am extremely grateful to them both. I have often wondered what the situation would be like if I hadn't had that opportunity for verbalising my dreams and hopes. Their influence didn't stop there, either. When I eventually became the Vicar of St James', Brian and Rachel decided to become Anglicans, and joined the fellowship and the task with me. This was not a painless decision for them, and I valued their fellowship and partnership. Brian was a Churchwarden at St James' for seven formative years until his appointment in 1985 as the Head of the Prime Minister's Policy Unit.

During these past years in Muswell Hill it has been my privilege to have some very special friends who have been prepared to give practical support when necessary and words of caution when I was in danger of steaming ahead with a half-formed idea. Brian and Rachel were typical of this group and, as I've indicated, were especially helpful in those very early months when the real situation couldn't be divulged to any other people living in either of the two parishes. There were two things I particularly valued from my friendship with Brian. Uppermost was his encouragement. He has a great respect for the church and its leadership. He kept me afloat when I felt like sinking and on course when I might have strayed—but always with grace and generosity. I had never known such support until then. I am sure others were eager to give it, but Brian verbalised it so often and enthusiastically that I believed him. We didn't always agree on everything, but I never felt he was manipulating me as I felt some tried to do.

The second thing I valued was Brian's critical mind. He has that amazing ability to get to the heart of an issue. If I ever felt in a fog over something, a chat with Brian usually blew it away and clarified what had to be done. Although it was often Brian with whom I shared most things, as we tossed them around together Rachel was no sleeping partner. She also had the ability to see the real issues. What she said would sometimes clarify and confirm the conclusions we had come to, or put a spanner in the works, forcing us to get back to the starting line again. They never put the matter behind them if it wasn't properly concluded. Brian and Rachel's help, and God's leading, meant that the vital process of linking the two parishes was achieved with remarkably few problems. When we formulated our decisions we also looked at the possible reactions to them. Thus not only did I know what to do, but also how to react to the various groups within the church when the time actually came. I was therefore able to handle the situations with a degree of confidence which I had never known before. When challenged, which I was from time to time, and even when I was criticised, which wasn't too unusual either in the first couple of years, I was able to respond without seriously polarising the situation and becoming defensive. What was even more important was that those hours with Brian and Rachel helped to build my sense of personal assurance, enabling me to avoid, to a large degree, wrongly interpreting criticism of a decision as a personal attack on me.

Remarkably, all through this frustrating period there was only one occasion when I felt that criticism was directed at me personally. That was at a time when I was feeling particularly low and vulnerable. We had had a disastrous family holiday. It had been far from relaxing and restful, and the children, now well into their teens, hadn't really enjoyed it either. In addition, it hadn't been cheap—which irritated us no end! There were a number of key people at St James' who were questioning whether I was leading the church in the opposite direction to that in which it really should be going. They made it known that they were seriously considering forming a lobby to stop me. I went to the Bishop feeling my world was about to collapse! He quickly brought me back to an even keel, pointing out that anything which wasn't inspired by God would soon evaporate—which it did. These ripples of discontent were actually so small that the vast majority of the church probably never heard them. It was my fault to blow up out of proportion a small query by a minority. How often the devil uses this tactic. He makes us think that the whole world is against us when actually just a few people are understandably anxious about a situation and not against us at all. In this case, the people's reaction sprang out of a loving concern for their church, and they just needed reassurance and convincing that we were on the right track.

So it was that soon after lunch one afternoon the Bishop telephoned to tell me he was now able to offer me the 'living'. I think I said 'yes' right away. On reflection, I probably should have said, 'Let me pray about it, then I'll give you my answer.' But the truth was that I had thought and prayed about little else, or so it seemed, for weeks. I was so thrilled that I had to tell Mary straightaway. As she was on one of her stints at the Royal Free Hospital, and I couldn't discover which ward she was on, I walked to Hampstead and managed to meet her on her way home. Our feet didn't touch the ground for several days with excitement. At last it was going to happen. If the truth is known, I've actually lived in something of that state of euphoria for the past eight years, even in the most difficult moments. St. James' is a truly remarkable church and to be its vicar is a tremendous privilege.

One lasting memory I have of the period just before my institution as the Vicar of St James' is the tremendous confidence the people of St Matthew's had in me. At a special meeting for the whole parish, I shared my

vision for the new situation. I was to become the new
Vicar of St James', and I hoped and prayed that the
people of St Matthew's would move with me from the
very first Sunday. I hoped that we could agree to
worship together and from then onwards work together
too. I shall never forget that meeting. Both young and
old voted to move and never to use St Matthew's
church buildings again but to sell the site and invest in
the new opportunity. I wasn't surprised by the enthusiasm of the younger members of the congregation.
What was so inspiring was the vision and sense of
sacrifice our older members had. These folk had
actually been involved in the building of the church,
and most had attended the Grand Opening and Dedi-
cation in 1940.

Mrs Wynne Brown was typical of this older genera-
tion. She and her husband had brought up their family
in the life of St Matthew's. She had seen her children
baptised, confirmed and married there and her
husband's funeral service took place there. She had
been one of the core members who had helped to raise
the parish's part of the funds necessary to build the
vicarage some fifteen years earlier. Yet she was prepared to move—to agree to the church being pulled
down for the sake of the future growth and development
of the church in Muswell Hill. And she is still with us,
even though she has to be brought to church through
the 'lift' system we started the moment we moved, for
she is now frail and elderly. I am sure she would agree
that the experience of the past eight years has really
challenged and strengthened her faith. The years
haven't been easy for her—family illness and problems
have abounded, yet there she is Sunday by Sunday.

It is with happy memories, too, that I recall Daisy

Madge, a very quaint unmarried lady with a heart of gold. A pillar of St Matthew's for many years, she really welcomed the new young people into the church there and appreciated the life they brought as well as the help they gave her. She was a visionary and enthusiastically supported the move to St James' and the selling of the site upon which much of her spiritual life had been nurtured. She relished the developing life at St James', giving it all the support she could. Long before the move she had decided to leave her house and belongings in her will to the Vicar and Churchwardens of St Matthew's. When she heard of the vision for the 'Church on the Hill', she decided to leave her house to the Vicar and Churchwardens of St James' instead. She wanted to give the new venture every support. She hadn't much to give in terms of ready cash, but she so wanted the new church to have her house and belongings when she died.

What a wonderful gift this has been! Thanks to dear Daisy and her vision we have been able to house another member of staff to help further the pastoral work of the church. But for her generosity we would have had to find something like £70 or £80,000 to buy such a house in Muswell Hill. I am so glad that she was able to see something of the fruit of her vision in her own lifetime, before she was taken from us in November 1985. She often used to whisper to me in the early days of the move, 'Isn't it all exciting?' And so it was. It could so easily have been spoilt by negative, cautious attitudes. Instead, positive affirmations helped to push us forward into this new and challenging opportunity. The present church owes a great deal to such folk.

The service which launched us all into the new

phase in the life of the church was very exciting. Although I was at the centre of the service in many respects, being 'Collated and Instituted' as the technical language of the Church of England puts it, I nevertheless felt that it was not just a new job for me and a new man for the parish, but more importantly a new chapter for the whole church. I saw the service as not simply placing me in a job, but opening this new chapter. The church was packed, including almost all the clergy from the local area who came to give their support and crowds of folk from Muswell Hill who came to witness this new beginning. The Bishop was marvellous. Speaking on the need for vision and change, he sparkled with wit and enthusiasm and we all sensed that this was a very special event.

My own feelings were mixed. I felt rather out of my depth, as I always have done ever since that evening. I couldn't believe that people, never mind God, could trust me to do such a big job. St James' could become a crucial church in the area, but would I fluff it and make a fool of myself? I wasn't unduly worried by the latter as I had become used to doing that, but I was far more concerned about the former. St Matthew's folk had given up their independence as a congregation, trusting that I would look after their interests and make sure the sacrifice was not in vain. St James' congregation had done the same, and in addition it had never had a vicar with such limited experience. Its previous incumbents had been men of standing and proven ability in the Church of England. In spite of these things, there wasn't a hint of uncertainty or anxiety in the atmosphere of that evening service. I felt the full support of the whole congregation and that has continued ever since. The Bishop, perhaps more than all of us, had taken the biggest risk. He knew me better than most, yet there wasn't a hint of uncertainty from him, but rather bouyant optimism.

I am so thankful to God that these supportive people have not been, by and large, disappointed. I knew that this new era in the life of the church would make demands upon us all. I faced the challenge of changing my style of leadership over the next few years as the church grew. But above all else on that evening I was conscious of the Lord's presence. It was his work, his church, his people and the vision was surely his too. I knew that he was with me. I wanted to build the church like Paul, 'the master builder'. I wanted to see folk coming to Christ, coming to his church and identifying with his work. His particular word to me then was, 'I am with you.' What is more, I knew that he would never leave me either, for that is his promise. The Lord had been faithful and I knew that I could trust him further as we ventured forth in faith. The simple challenge to me, as it is to us all, was to be faithful.

4

A People of Worship

Now I was actually Vicar of the 'Church on the Hill', I had to consider how to help it move from depression and decline to vibrancy and new life. How could I help to form a warm fellowship, a real community of God's people who were regularly and enthusiastically involved in worship and mission?

A number of key areas would have to change. One of them was worship. I firmly believe that worship is critical to the whole of our lives. The quality of our worship can and does affect our daily walk with Christ, our sense of belonging to our fellow Christians, and our vision for God's kingdom and what we should be doing to help bring it about.

Ever since I first experienced God's grace and love so freely given in his Son, I have always felt under an obligation to tell others about him. This is a distinctive characteristic of evangelical Christians. While the importance of worship has always been a conviction of mine, over the years at St James' this has deepened and intensified. We have an obligation to worship this God of love and grace. What has helped me to see this has been a growing appreciation of the link between evangelism and worship.

Dr Jim Packer, in *The Evangelical Anglican Identity Problem* (Oxford: Latimer, 1978), comments on the priority of evangelism:

> What the joy of being found does for an evangelical is to drive him out to find others. His wish to share Christ seems to him natural and normal. He knows himself to be under orders to go as a witness for Christ and make disciples and he finds himself wanting to do it... Peter says that God's people are to "declare the wonderful deeds of him who called you out of darkness into his marvellous light" (1 Peter 2:10). When asked if these words relate to worshipping God or witnessing to men, evangelicals would say, both, and to identify the second as an aspect of the first.

Douglas Webster, in his much under-rated little book *Local Church and World Mission* makes a similarly helpful point. In New Testament thinking, worship and mission keep running into each other—they belong together. Liturgy enjoins mission and is the inspiration for mission.

John Stott makes the connection between these two main occupations of the apostolic church—worship and mission—even clearer. In his book *Our Guilty Silence* (London: Hodder and Stoughton) he shows that worship involves witness and witness involves worship. He writes:

> Each is maimed without the other. Each, if true to itself, leads to the other, thus producing an unending cycle. Worship expresses itself in witness; witness fulfils itself in worship. The unifying theme is the glory of God and of His Christ.

It was clear to me that if my dream and vision for the church was to be realised, more and more people won for Christ and more disciples made, then Sunday worship would have to be high on my list of priorities. I would have to give a good deal of my time to planning and preparing for it, and I would also have to review it constantly. This still holds true today.

I decided that some basic changes needed to be made in the pattern of worship at St James'. Few people would have described the worship during the interregnum as inspiring. Indeed, when the news of my appointment became public, the Area Dean, the Rev Clifford Doyle, telephoned to congratulate me on my appointment and wish me well. He also confessed that he found those times when he had led the worship at St James' as some of the most depressing moments of his ministry. I knew what he meant. Clifford was from the Anglo-Catholic tradition, while St James' was 'low'. It hadn't the colour and mystery of the Anglo-Catholic tradition, nor the marks of an evangelical ministry. Very few of the members were excited by what happened Sunday by Sunday — it just seemed to happen. For some the fire of enthusiasm and eagerness still burned brightly, and the church owes a great deal to these people for its present vitality.

One of the elements that was missing at St Matthew's and which I felt weakened many aspects of its life, including worship, was a sense of tradition. It had a reasonably good grasp of the contemporary scene and the present-day challenges that it faced, but it had little sense that it was building on the foundation of a great tradition which could enrich its developing life. St Matthew's resembled a typical college or university Christian union whose membership changes virtually every three years. The concern of these important centres of Christian witness is not so much to build a worshipping, stable Christian community, but simply to be a fellowship of keen Christians who are eager to grow in the faith themselves and share it with others. I suspect that many of our young members—and they were in the majority—had a vision for St Matthew's which was largely modelled on the fellowship which they had experienced in those Christian unions in their student days.

I believe that tradition is important. I greatly valued many of the traditions at St James' that had helped to hold the church together during its darker years. I wanted to keep them, develop them and build upon them, leaving an even richer tradition for future generations of Christians. Of course, this vision for the church had to be complemented by that shared by our younger members from St Matthew's. The church also had to be truly contemporary: it had to be fully involved in society as an influential force for good, and it also had to have an evangelistic impact on the community.

It is easy to fall into the trap of treating these two visions of the church as mutually exclusive. Those who appreciate the value of roots and traditions may have no time for those who want the church to be con-temporary, while those who regard the church as a contemporary community may see little place for tradition and continuity. When camps are formed by these two groups of people within the church, the strategy of the church's life and work is put in jeopardy. I wanted to help those with a sense of tradition to come to a proper understanding of the contemporary work of the church, and similarly to help those who identified with the church as a contemporary force to appreciate the importance of tradition and heritage in the church's developing life. I hoped that a growing number of people would be able to hold these two aspects in tension, for I felt that the church would be richer and more stable as a consequence.

When it came to the area of worship, I knew that I was dealing with a very important and sensitive subject to Christians. Most people have views on this subject and very few are diffident in expressing them. Change would have to be introduced very carefully.

Certainly in our congregation, and I suspect in most, we have some people who enjoy variety. They would love every service to be as totally different from the one before as it could be. Hardly anything within the service is sacrosanct to them. When it comes to change they are prepared to consider changing any- thing and everything—the dress, the lights, the furni- ture, the time, the leadership, the words, the actions— everything. Then there are others who are the very opposite. When it comes to change you can almost see them visibly withdraw. The very word seems to do something to them. If the choice is 'change or decay' they would rather die gracefully with the known, than venture forth into the unknown!

As so often happens, the voice of reason and balance doesn't get heard because those in the camps at the two extremes get together and become locked in combat. The secret seems to be to win the main body of those folk who, while quite keen on change and developing relevant worship, can see the value of the fixed points and some tradition. These folk can then help avert the all too frequent polarisation that takes place the moment anything new is suggested.

In suggesting change in worship, I have found it helpful to set a trial period with a review at the end. This avoids getting into defensive positions with people. My approach has always been, by and large, conciliatory. If something doesn't work, then we drop it—even if it was originally my idea. We have dropped quite a number over the years!

I believe that worship should have a real note of celebration and festivity, and we need to be prepared to implement changes that will bring this about as painlessly and effectively as possible. To those deeply rooted in the great traditions of the church, we must affirm our commitment to moving along well-travelled and approved roads while pointing out that we live in a rapidly changing world and that our church is very diverse in its membership—people whom *God* has brought to faith and to such membership. To those at the other extreme who would like to throw out all traditions and have something new and different every Sunday, we must affirm our commitment to being truly contemporary, 'where people are'. But we must point out the need to learn from the past, to note what God has blessed, and to keep some fixed points in worship. A liturgical structure provides a framework for this. Once it is dispensed with we can so easily fall into all sorts of dangers.

While on a sabbatical study leave in California, I visited a large well-known church for their communion service. There were two collections but no specific Bible reading as such, although thankfully a brief Bible passage was referred to in the sermon. There was no creed or affirmation of congregational faith. Of course, this was only one service on one Sunday, but if it was typical then to my mind it was a slippery slope.

The Christian content was already very thin and could so easily become even non-Christian if left to develop like this.

The benefits of a liturgy are enormous, one being that it helps to keep us on track. To be guided simply by desire—what folk like best—will result in impoverished worship. We have to keep in mind that the prime reason for coming together as a church is to please God and worship *him*, and our worship should reflect something of his greatness and worthiness.

I reviewed the traditions of the two churches and tried to bring them together in a pattern of weekly worship that would not be unfamiliar to either. I also tried to provide a pattern of worship for the present community in Muswell Hill, rather than for the dead or those not yet born! The folk at St Matthew's were used to informal worship much of the time, especially in their monthly Family Services. St James', on the other hand, was much more conservative. Informal services were only held very occasionally. Most of the services were from the Prayer Book with some use of Series 2. The Psalms and Canticles as well as the Versicles and Responses were chanted and sung and the *English Hymnal* was the congregational hymn book. St Matthew's hadn't chanted anything for a number of years, and the responses, when used, were said, *Psalm Praise* and *Christian Praise* were the sources for all the hymns. Both churches were used to a monthly cycle of Morning Prayer and Holy Communion services.

Whatever monthly pattern we eventually adopted and whatever liturgy we decided to use, my only hope was that peoples' aspirations would be immediately raised. The process of making this decision was both careful and prayerful. Once I had made a draft plan I called together the Churchwardens and Readers from both churches to discuss it. I proposed that it should be implemented from my first Sunday. At this meeting, which was very amicable and positive, I also shared my hopes for the church and my desire that the draft plan would be the way forward. I asked for any insights and comments, both positive and negative, and the final plan was then agreed, virtually as I had proposed. The monthly plan of evening services and the liturgy used were to remain more or less as they had been at St James' for some years.

Every Sunday evening we would have Evening Prayer from the Prayer Book except on one Sunday in the month when we would have a full Holy Communion service. My suggestion was that we should use the Prayer Book liturgy for this Holy Communion, but surprisingly they decided that we should use Series 3. The other difference was that I suggested we should use the Prayer Book liturgy and Series 3 on alternate-Sundays at the 8.00 am service. This was agreed upon after some discussion, but when we sought to implement it I quickly realised that it was far better to use only the Prayer Book for this early morning service and we have done this ever since.

The final monthly plan of services was as follows:

8.00 am	Holy Communion (every week) (BCP)
11.00 am	1st Sunday MP (BCP)
	2nd Sunday MP (Series 3)
	3rd Sunday HC (Series 3)
	4th Sunday Family Service (using some sections of the Series 3 service)

| 6.30 pm | Evening Prayer (BCP) except the 1st Sunday |
| | 1st Sunday   Holy Communion (Series 3) |

Along with these changes to the main services I made another proposal concerning Children's Church — a service for the children led by children in church every Sunday. This had been running for several years and had been well attended but it was now in decline. The church was, however, too weak in a number of areas to run three services every Sunday morning; an 8.00 am Holy Communion, 10.00 am Children's Church, and 11.00 am Morning Prayer. A plan was accepted to bring the whole church family together at 11.00 am and then provide teaching groups for the children to go to after about fifteen minutes of adult worship.

The Evening Service was the slowest to grow numerically. This didn't surprise me at all. It was almost extinct as a viable service when I arrived. Few Anglican churches in London have a regular evening service today. The evening congregation I inherited looked lost in our vast building. To organise inspiring worship for some 30 or 40 people in a building that holds over 700 was an uphill task. But it did slowly change.

In those early days I concentrated on preaching and congregational singing. I decided to make the Evening Service in particular a major opportunity for teaching.

What is expected from the English pulpit is considerable, and how we can get anywhere near it without a great deal of hard work I just do not know. Unlike America where there is a long tradition of adult Bible classes, our teaching of the faithful has to be done largely through the Sunday sermon. I suspect that for far too many this is their main biblical meal of the week, if not their only biblical meal. I fail to see how this can be given in just five minutes or even ten. Christians brought up on such a meagre diet will not become strong and healthy, able to cope with the challenges that come to most Christians at some time or other, such as redundancy, illness or bereavement. The devil can so easily turn these difficult situations into temptations to fall away from the faith. They will certainly not be able to 'give a reason for the hope that is within them' unless such insubstantial nourishment is supported by other opportunities for learning, which it rarely is.

No company that is eager to stay in business and sell its product would dream of giving such scant training and support as we give our members. The commanding officer wouldn't entertain the idea of sending his soldiers into hand-to-hand contact with a dangerous and difficult foe on the front line without giving them the instruction and practice that would give them the self-confidence and ability to defend themselves and assure them of survival and victory. Yet so often this is just what the church does.

I have tried not to fall into this trap, as I am aware that the pressures facing Christians today are considerable. I have also tried to avoid the opposite danger of giving people so much that they do not take in anything. This is a very difficult balance to strike, one I have failed to achieve on many occasions.

My approach is to be shorter and more popular in style for the morning congregation, bearing in mind the kind of folk who come. I aim towards twenty minutes maximum, but often give more. A regular influx of fringe people and newcomers come to this service. In the evening we spread our wings a little, being slightly longer and deeper and expecting more from the hearers. In our case this isn't an unreasonable expectation. The encouraging fact is that both the morning and the evening congregations have grown steadily on this approach.

Very early on at St James' we agreed that a new emphasis should be placed upon the sermon. I explained to the worshipping community why I saw this part of my ministry as important, and that it would need time for preparation and implementation within the service—it couldn't be done properly in ten minutes. I have found it very helpful to plan the services and my sermons well in advance. This involves looking carefully at the spiritual state of the church, diagnosing the most crucial need or pressing problem, and selecting scripture which will give a relevant and helpful exposition—in my view one of the most demanding tasks of the ministry. Planning has helped us provide, over the years, a balanced biblical diet and eventually, we hope, a full coverage of Scripture. I give the congregation prior notice of themes and subjects, providing them with a sermon card for each service.

My sermons are in fact more what I would term Bible readings. Remembering my college days with Alan Stibbs and F D Kidner, I choose a book from the Old or New Testament and work through the text, expounding and applying it, trying to give both a pastoral and evangelistic thrust. To be as true to Scripture as possible, I try to expound texts and subjects which are challenging, humbling and deeply searching. But I believe that these must be handled in such a way that the congregation returns home uplifted no matter how much they have been challenged by a fresh consciousness of their failure and sin. I believed then, as I do now, that the prime purpose of teaching in our worship is to build up, to edify, and that this can only be achieved by thorough and careful exposition of Scripture.

I enjoyed preparing my Bible readings, and slowly people came and took an interest in what was being given. They even started to bring their Bibles to church! It was hard to keep up a reasonable standard as most of the time I was preaching twice on Sunday. This was a deliberate policy, for I derived great pleasure from preaching—trying to shed light on God's word and showing its relevance to our everyday life. From the very beginning I wanted to take every opportunity to turn the heads of the congregation from a survival mentality to expansion and development. Every Sunday was of critical importance in this.

One particular series of Bible readings was especially helpful in building up the evening worshipping community. It was nothing very unusual or original. It was a series on the Apostles' Creed entitled 'I Believe'. However, I asked a number of reasonably well-known people to come and preach on the various sections of the Creed, together with myself and Brian Griffiths. Our visitors included such people as The Rev Dick Lucas from St Helen's, Bishopsgate, David Winter from the BBC, Sir Fred Catherwood, and the then Bishop of Edmonton, Bill Westwood, all of whom were particularly challenging. We organised a 'feed-back' session with the preachers afterwards in the vicarage. The whole series produced a good deal of interest, as have others since.

However over the years since I became vicar we have had few visiting preachers. While some of them have been very well known in church circles, their reputation has not been widespread among the relatively unchurched—their names certainly lacked the drawing power that I thought they would have. Our own 'special services' of one kind or another seemed to have a greater attraction. However, these visitors have made a very positive contribution and I have greatly appreciated their help and support. In the early days they relieved the pressure on me when I was on my own, and some of the especially gifted preachers did reach people whom we had failed to reach, though we might have tried week in, week out. I am not sure that having these visiting preachers has contributed significantly to numerical growth, yet some folk in our congregation have made a great surge forward in their spiritual development through the ministry of one or other of our distinguished visitors. We are privileged today to have preachers and teachers who are equipped by God to reach and teach the 'flock', as well as being powerful evangelists.

I believe that music is also critical to inspiring worship. It can make or mar a service. A positive, rousing tune supporting words that speak of God's majesty and glory encourages people in their praise and adoration, releasing them to bring their emotions into the offering of themselves to God. If the tune is very well known then most if not all the congregation are brought together in expressing praise to God. This is very uplifting. Of course, the opposite can happen. An unknown or difficult tune, however good its words, can result in a dull service that enthusiastic leadership from the front has great difficulty in overcoming.

Any church is full of different people who vary in the kind of music they find helpful in worship. For this reason we try to ensure that most musical tastes are catered for without swinging to any extremes. This has been a gradual process, but people of widely differing musical preferences now feel able to worship God through a variety of music. One thing is sure—we are not in the business of trying to educate people's musical taste. If we were to do that we would run the risk of making music the focal point and not worship. Music must never become a hindrance to worship and so needs to be broadly acceptable and readily under-stood by those who come into the church, particularly for the first time. For this reason we rarely have the spontaneous singing of a song as this will inevitably exclude those who are unfamiliar with it.

In 1985 we produced our own song book. This is a collection of modern Christian songs culled from many of the books on the market at that time. The process of obtaining the appropriate copyright permissions was costly and time consuming. Happily the publishers have now made better arrangements for dealing with this problem. We now pay an annual sum which allows us to copy and use a wide range of new songs that have become available since the printing of our own book. These modern songs are mostly accom-panied by a small group of singers and musicians, though the organ often gives back-up.

In introducing the modern we have not neglected the old. As well as our traditional choir of about fourteen adults and twelve boys who sing a wide range of choral works, we have a small choir of eight who sing some of the madrigal repertoire, often unaccom-panied, during the administration of the evening Holy

Communion service. From time to time these regular groups of musicians are augmented by others from the congregation to perform larger works ranging from traditional ones such as a Bach cantata to a modern musical extravaganza by Roger Jones.

For congregational singing we use the *Anglican Hymn Book* in the morning together with *Psalm Praise*. In the evening we have the additional possibilities of *Hymns for Today's Church* as well as our own song book.

The organist at St James' when I became vicar was a fine gentleman and a musician of distinction, who had been organist at St James' for fifty-four years. I believe that he had chosen the hymns and chants and played a prominent role in the leading and character of the Sunday worship for all this time. I felt that it was too much to ask a man in his eightieth year, after fifty-four years of one style of worship, to adopt a very different one.

Once the news of my appointment was public, I heard that he was eager to see me, so I suggested we had a chat, at the end of which I said that I felt I had to look for another organist to carry on the work he had founded. I indicated that I would endeavour to make sure that he could keep on with his practice and teaching which was in great demand. I said that I hoped he would play at my Institution, but from then onwards I really felt the church needed someone else. He seemed to be shocked by all this, which didn't surprise me, but he behaved like the gentleman he was. Ever since that interview I have sought to keep my promise of practice and teaching time, though it has had to be reduced somewhat because of increasing demands on the use of the church and the organ itself, and during these years we have maintained an amicable relationship.

Unfortunately, once this news was made public it created a stir both in the local press and the organists' world which eventually affected the congregation of St James'. There was a crisis of confidence. A special PCC meeting was called and two proposals were made. First, that the present organist continue in his post for a further six months after which the issue of his replacement could be discussed again. Secondly, that the proposed changes to the services mentioned above should not be implemented until after my Institution and a full discussion with the PCC. I wasn't a member of that PCC at that time, of course, so I could not attend. Providentially, both proposals were defeated.

Looking back, I believe that the changes that were made even before I took up office were crucial to the future life of the church. I was then, and still am, very grateful to God for the courage he gave me to weather the storm. In fact, it might be better described as simply a small cloud in the clear sky, for once I was installed and we got underway, those decisions were never questioned and since then no one has ever said to me that they were unwise.

Once the word was out that we were without an organist I had a queue of most capable musicians itching to have a go on our fine instrument, designed by the previous organist and built and installed by Harrison and Harrison of Durham. I was looking for a permanent organist who would be able to uphold the high standards established over the years and to lead, support and inspire the worship.

During the interim I was very conscious of God's care and provision for us. We were able to keep things going with some sense of style and quality. Tim

Marshall had been on Sunday placement with me while he was an ordinand studying at Oak Hill Theological College. I had asked that he might continue with us at St James' and they agreed to this. Among his many talents Tim was a capable organist, having been the organist at St Mary's, Islington, before training for ordination. We managed with only a few 'hairy' moments to keep things going until Alan Horsey arrived to fill the vacant post of Organist and Musical Director.

Alan was with us for about seven years. I look back on this period as a very special time. He quickly became a close friend, and right from the start he shared my vision for the worship. Alan had a real talent in leading congregational worship and was a sensitive and flexible musician. No matter what he was playing, it was invariably an inspiration and encouragement to the congregation while still being music of real quality. He contributed a great deal in helping to bridge the gap between the old days of St James' and the new era of 'St-James'—with— St-Matthew's'. Alan left us in 1985 to take up the post of organist and choir master at Bradford Cathedral.

Thankfully, God has provided us with another—like the first. Simon Over shares Alan's ability and rare spiritual commitment to the work, qualities missing in so many otherwise fine organists. While he was still finishing his studies at Oxford we had the support of an able deputy, Jeremy Allen, who continues to assist Simon now he is working full time with us. We have been greatly blessed by these musicians. We have a helpful choir and a number of folk who can either form an orchestra or simply play as individual instrumentalists augmenting the organ. We have come a long way in the past few years.

For some years now we have been singing certain parts of the Communion Service. During this time we have only had one setting which we have sung twice a month, once in the morning and once in the evening. No one from the congregation has ever complained that he is tired of it. The value of regularly singing familiar music in this way is that people are able to concentrate upon the words more easily as they sing them. When we come to the Gloria, for example, everyone becomes deeply involved and the singing takes on new vigour and volume. One of my proposals concerning the services at St James' was that we would not chant the canticles or Psalms but find alternative music and say the responses. We purchased 200 copies of *Psalm Praise* and used them to supplement our musical resources. However, I would dearly love to find some suitable music that would enable us once again to sing these tremendous Old and New Testament songs and Psalms. *Psalm Praise*, in spite of its musical shortcomings in some people's opinion, has still helped us enormously.

From my very first Sunday at St James' my earlier thoughts about the church's rich potential have been confirmed. Since then every Sunday has been full of excitement for me. But I realised from the beginning that this sense of excitement in worship would have to be kept alive by variety as well as enthusiasm. The Anglican calendar provides marvellous opportunities for special services. To these we have also added others of our own. In the main morning service these have tended to be on the more formal side, such as an Advent Festival, a Festival of Carols at Christmas, Mothering Sunday, Whit Sunday, our Patronal Festival and Trinity Sunday.

In the evening we have been more adventurous. Very rarely is one service exactly the same as another—the individual ingredients vary considerably from month to month. To our normal cycle of services we have recently added a Spotlight Service. The main aim of this is to reach the under thirty-fives. We first tried a series of monthly Spotlight Services as an experiment for three months at the end of 1985. An additional intention was to give some of our lay folk a chance to use and develop the gifts and abilities God had given them in speaking and leading in worship.

The first three were: Spotlight on the Father, Spotlight on the Son, and Spotlight on the Holy Spirit. The effort put into these services by the three teams responsible was well rewarded. The services were such a success that we decided to continue them. We are now in our third year of these Spotlight Services and we have seen a considerable increase in the size of the evening congregation from about 120 to 170.

In planning our regular services, I have tried to keep in mind that one of the main objectives of the church is worship. The Apostle Peter described the church as a 'spiritual house' made of 'living stones' created supremely to God's glory and in order to worship him (1 Pet 2). The thought of the Lamb once slain and now glorified will surely draw Christians out to seek every opportunity to give our God and Redeemer what we owe him and what we desire to offer him. I suspect that one of the main reasons for the apparent apathy towards and neglect of public worship can be traced to a lack of understanding and appreciation of the cross of Christ. Peter explains: 'Once [we] were not a people, but now [we] are the people of God;

once [we] had not received mercy, but now [we] have received mercy' (1 Pet 2:10). All this is, of course, through Jesus Christ. I have also tried not to forget the worshippers themselves and that God will be wanting to bless them and meet with them in the worship. Hopefully, the worship will be both God-centred and truly enriching for all present. This is a great challenge. I have prayed that through our worship the individual members of the congregation may move forward to a further point of maturity and spiritual experience, as well as enjoy and benefit from being in the presence of God. It has been most heartening over the years to see many develop in this way. For some this has been a slow and gradual change from a rather formal quiet faith to something more vibrant which has become of central importance rather than merely casual and occasional. For others it has been much more dramatic, or even traumatic.

John and Janet Smith (these are not their real names but pseudonyms) were married in 1964 in one of our neighbouring Anglican churches where both before and after their marriage they were heavily involved in the work of the church. In 1966 they moved to Muswell Hill but didn't move churches until 1970 when their children began to attend St James' School where they as parents had become very involved. They had begun to feel strongly that it was right to worship in the community in which they lived, so they came to St James'.

It wasn't long before they became leaders of the young people's fellowship, members of the PCC, and Janet became a Sunday school teacher. All was well for some years but underneath they both felt a lack of spiritual development. This was voiced on a number of occasions and people began to suggest that perhaps they should move to a church where they would be happier.

John was the first to leave in 1974, attracted by the fast-growing house church movement which had a 'branch' in the area. Janet was more cautious, being loath to leave the Sunday school teaching she loved, but eventually she felt convicted that her place was with her husband. At first the freedom was quite wonderful—they described it as 'floating around on a spiritual high'. They enjoyed the unstructured meetings, marvellous teaching and preaching, and constantly uplifting times of praise. It was all so exciting, and in their view they grew more spiritually in a few months than they had done in the whole of their previous Christian experience.

It took about a year for things to go sour. Individually and as a couple they became the object of authoritarian leadership attention: they should not be sending their three children to a church school; they argued with the other members of the house church too much (and were given a recently married couple to counsel them); it was wrong for Janet to continue working part-time at St James' playgroup as a mother's place was in the home; their frequent hospitality to others in their house was seen as an attempt to establish a hold over them...and so it went on. Worst of all they began to query, both privately and directly with those concerned, whether some of this 'instruction' was right. They were told they had a 'rebellious spirit' and that their leaders, though much younger than they, were appointed by God and must not be challenged.

The crunch came for each of them separately. John was told by a leader that he and his wife's hospitality could not be accepted until they were able to accept the leadership's authority. Janet was told, on the day following her father's death, that she was possessed. She was prayed over and 'delivered'—of what she never discovered—and John was never consulted or involved. Such authoritarian attitudes were just too much for them both, and after a 'trial separation' they eventually left that house church late in 1976 spiritually and emotionally crippled. I want to emphasise that this is their, not my, assessment of their experience.

After a while their children started to attend the Sunday school at another nearby church, and in time they began worshipping there themselves. As was not the case when they made their original move to St James', they were left alone and allowed to settle in—a number of people knew what they had been through. It was their own decision to become more involved. They became members in 1977, Janet became a Sunday school teacher and John a Covenanter leader. But they again seemed to become isolated because they were unhappy about the lack of spiritual growth. They seemed to be the chief advocates of discontent, but they had learned enough in previous years to know that if they were to stay they should support the leadership. Again, John left first, followed by Janet a few months later in 1982. Together with a few others they became founder members of a new house church in North London.

During 1982 their previous experience with the house church repeated itself. Despite marvellous times of praise and teaching they encountered the same problems of authoritarian attitudes which could not and should not be challenged. After yet more traumatic confrontations, they both saw the writing on the wall early enough to leave before too much damage was done. So they left at the end of 1982, wondering what was wrong with them. Were they really rebellious and set on wanting things their own way? Were they even meant to be involved in a church at all?

For a while they went nowhere, other than the occasional visit to places like St Helen's, Bishopsgate, and to churches where constant and faithful Christian friends invited them. But the feeling of isolation overwhelmed them again. They knew that they should be involved somewhere, but where? They felt that they had been everywhere in the area. Their testimony continues:

> One night in mid-1983 we decided to visit St James', and were amazed by what we saw. We knew that the church had started to grow again, but had no idea to what extent. True authoritative spiritual leadership was evident, but not in an overbearing way. Folk had real spiritual hunger, and entire families were coming along. Bible study groups were meeting, and people were talking to each other about their faith and their Lord. So we continued to come, grateful just to find Christian friendship and growth. Some were intrigued by our return, and were clearly a little afraid of us. But we understood and didn't mind, fully accepting that we were not to be involved in any sort of leadership—we were still getting to know our family again.

Some time in mid-1984 I wrote to the Smiths, asking them to come and see me and talk about their involvement with us. I had known them personally since we first came to Muswell Hill in 1970, through the school. I was concerned for them. They looked lost, but I didn't want to encourage what appeared to be a

Christian 'gad-fly' attitude, flitting from one church to another.

I talked frankly to them about my anxieties and emphasised how important I considered church membership to be and that it was not something to be treated lightly. They sat and listened and shared their experiences as I have outlined them above. I suggested that they consider carefully and prayerfully whether or not they wanted to become regular worshippers with us, pointing out that I didn't feel I would be able to give them any position of real leadership in the church for at least a couple of years, even though they had been Christians longer than many of our folk, thus giving them time to prove themselves. Closing our meeting with prayer for both them and the church, I suggested that they come to see me again if they did decide to stay and become involved. I was touched by their humility as they left.

John and Janet did decide to stay. They were patient and gracious, and are now well-respected as well as stable members of our fellowship. I have a great regard for them both. They openly acknowledge the mistakes they have made in wanting a perfect church, and have become faithful supporters of the work and worship at St James'.

It was our Sunday worship that first made John and Janet look again at St James'. I am delighted that these folk and others like them, with different stories to tell, have been restored to regular worship and church involvement.

The size of our committed Sunday worshipping family has grown in a steady rather than dramatic way. But when one compares the situation in 1977 with the situation now in 1988, the difference is marked. In 1977 the main sections of the chancel were just sprinkled with people whereas the chancel now looks full if not crowded and the two sides are also beginning to fill up. We look forward to the day when they too are, week by week, crowded with eager worshippers!

5

Family and Fellowship

Although Sunday worship provides a special occasion for the Christian church, its family life cannot possibly be sustained, let alone develop, on this alone. It is extremely difficult for true fellowship to take place in church on Sunday, even if you provide coffee as we and many others do. At the back of our church building there just isn't the room for the whole congregation to gather and share together after a service. Moreover, after the morning service most adults with families have to have one eye on what the children are up to and the other on the clock because of lunch and wider family responsibilites. The time after the evening service is somewhat more relaxed, and people tend to stay around a little longer. While this gives valuable opportunities for fellowship, it still cannot provide every member with the depth of fellowship that he needs. Furthermore, those with families simply cannot always be there.

When I got down to the concrete details of how to nurture the family and community life of the church, I found it helpful to remember that our church family consists of two general groups: the regulars and the newcomers. I have always seen coffee time after the sevice as an opportunity for welcoming the newcomers and, of course, any visitors. Over the past eight years we have tried to develop a ministry that is especially appropriate to these two general categories. Their needs may be similar but our ministry to them needs to be quite distinct until the newcomer becomes a regular or a committed member of the church family.

Before the move to St James' I had realised that the matter of fellowship would have to be treated with some care.

The people of St Matthew's would be leaving their roots and would therefore feel rather homeless. I would have to make a special effort to make sure that their new church became their spiritual home as soon as possible. While there were a number of people at St James' who had a real sense of belonging, this was by no means a widespread feeling. Generally speaking, people's special circle in the church was quite small.

I had decided that if the two congregations were to merge into one true fellowship rather than divide into groups of individuals, then I would have to try and begin a network of home Bible study fellowship groups.

What motivated me most in my thinking about the need for such small groups was the conviction that the church, the people of God, is by nature a fellowship. It therefore needs a structure to enable it to be what it is. I knew that this could never develop to any real degree on Sunday. The congregation had to be broken down into smaller units if the New Testament teaching on all-member mutual ministry was to be realised.

The New Testament teaches that we are to love one another, forgive one another, give hospitality to one another and carry one another's burdens. It is unrealistic and very frustrating to tell Christians to do this without giving them a basic structure within which they can begin. Some of the more outgoing members may perhaps make an attempt, but what of the vast majority of people who don't come into this category? Jesus himself began with a small circle of twelve disciples, and the New Testament is a constant reminder of what they learnt and achieved together.

Since starting our Bible Study Fellowship Groups we have discovered that other benefits have resulted over and above the aspect of fellowship. The groups give a futher Christian presence in the neighbourhood; they help in the training of leaders; they encourage Bible study and prayer; they help in the pastoral care of the congregation; they have become a channel of communication with the clergy; and they have provided small groups that can help in the leading of Sunday worship, as well as neighbourhood evangelism. But at the beginning I knew I couldn't jump straight into this. I was anxious about dividing people up into small groups early on because it would have been difficult to make sure the mix of each group was right. I wanted to avoid artificial groupings and certainly not to have St James' groups and St Matthew's groups. We needed situations in which the whole church could come together—young and old, regular and newcomer, St James' people and St Matthew's people. To achieve this my wife and I decided to keep on with our Sunday lunches. We did this for about a year, and it proved to be a most valuable time of fellowship each Sunday.

Keeping these lunches going wasn't at all easy. Although I was working from my study at St James' vicarage, the lunches had to be in St Matthew's vicarage, half a mile away. This was a great complication and I had to rely on Mary's help. Because of the extra work load and the fact that I was working 'away from home' in St James' vicarage, Mary had to give up her part-time nursing job which she had started two years earlier. We also began to divide up the work to make sure I didn't crack up under the pressure. I had additional commitments on Sundays which I had not had at St Matthew's. We did not have a verger, so I had to be in church much earlier before each service to ensure that all was ready. And with so many more people to get to know I had to stay by the door afterwards to greet people, so I couldn't rush off to see how the potatoes were doing!

The numbers coming to lunch grew—we frequently had between sixty and seventy with us. I well remember one Easter Sunday when I had been badly held up and lunch was delayed. With the extra pressure of this major festival, we had forgotten to put the peas on to boil. The consequent delay wouldn't have been a problem had it not been our custom at festivals to have a small glass of sherry before the meal. One of our elderly ladies, who rather liked the sherry, was beginning to get the worse for wear for she obviously hadn't eaten anything since early morning and folk had to ply her with biscuits to keep her on an even keel while we awaited the boiling of the peas. We very rarely have sherry now on such occasions!

These lunches also had an interesting by-product—publicity. Word had got out and the community was beginning to ask what went on on these occasions, what the menu was like, and whether the vicar was a good cook. The BBC *Woman's Hour* programme heard of it somehow and came along. They recorded me preparing on the Saturday morning, the actual building up to it on Sunday morning, and then stayed on through the service and to lunch afterwards. We all enjoyed their involvement but were rather staggered by the media interest following it. Photographs of me knee-deep in pans and cookery books appeared in a number of daily newspapers.

We had been running these lunches for about two months when a weekly newspaper got to hear of us. When they rang to see if they could write up a report and take some photographs, I was horrified to discover that the particular weekly was *Reveille!* Although this newspaper is no longer in circulation, I think it could fairly be described as not the best family reading. After taking advice I decided to go ahead. It has to be said that of all the reports we had to cope with, and some journalists do have a way of stretching the truth, theirs was a most sympathetic account. The only thing I didn't care for was their very corny captions to the photographs. Underneath one of me at the cooker: 'The shepherd feeds his flock'. Even worse, under another of a group of folk eating their lunch on our lawn: 'See them graze'.

Although hard work, these Sunday lunches were great fun and very rewarding. One faithful member of our church today, Beryl Scrutton, first came to us through hearing the *Woman's Hour* programme. A single lady, she appreciated what was provided and is now a committed Christian. Having tasted what we had to offer, she told a neighbour, Joyce Currie, in an adjoining flat. Joyce has also become a faithful member of the church, and when she married Graham Halliday in 1985 he became a regular worshipper with us too.

The Sunday lunches helped considerably in blending the two separate congregations into one family. Within a year or so we all considered ourselves to be one church.

There was a further reason why I felt that I couldn't go straight into the home Bible study groups. This was the thorny issue of the St James' folk's attitude to the Bible and its authority. While I believe that the Bible is able to reveal its own authority and therefore be let loose among the people, nevertheless, I felt it would be much more productive if in the first year of the merged church I dealt with the issue in a number of different ways and demonstrated the Bible's centrality to the church by giving it a prominent place in my ministry and in our Sunday worship. I didn't want a study group to spend all its time discussing whether or not the Bible ought to be read, but rather how to discern its principles and apply them to life.

Initially I tackled this through the regular Sunday preaching, but clearly this wasn't going to be sufficient. So I stopped the one Bible study I had inherited and started a Wednesday evening central study time. This took the form of a Bible reading and a time for open and extempore prayer. The latter was important as it is not only good to pray at every opportunity, but also vital to help as many as possible to express their concerns to God in this way.

From the outset this study group was quite well attended—we often managed a gathering of some thirty to forty people eagerly listening to God's word. It was a beginning. But at the same time I was keen to show that other people—people of good standing in the community—had a similar view of Scripture to my own. So I invited my friend Brian Griffiths to help me in this.

Brian was not only held in high esteem in our neighbourhood, but was also a respected academic and someone with a definite Christian commitment that most people soon became aware of. Happily for me he is a very fine preacher. He uses words graphically and speaks with a compelling Welsh *hwyl*. I enjoyed those Wednesday evenings of ministry together with Brian, and they seemed to have been appreciated for more and more people started to join us on a regular basis.

The time came, however, for us to move into the next phase and begin to form into Bible Study Fellowship Groups. At first we started just four groups meeting weekly with an occasional central meeting. But we soon discovered that people so valued their group that the central meeting began to lose its attractiveness. The obvious fact then dawned on me that the central meeting of the church is actually its Sunday worship. After about two years these four Bible Study Fellowship Groups became six.

The structure and programme for these groups are quite clear. They follow my division of the church year into three terms. Each term the individual groups are encouraged to include the following in their group life:

(1) Bible study and prayer—prayer diaries are often kept.
(2) Fellowship—the leaders and hosts organise various social activites.
(3) Once a term the three or four groups that form a Cluster group (see below) are encouraged to meet

together to enable people to get to know other members of the Cluster and of the church.

(4) Approximately once a term the groups are suspended so that we can all meet together for an evening of prayer. These have had ever-increasing support.

(5) Most of the groups are asked to host a meeting during the summer holiday period when normal group life is suspended. This also helps the group to get to know a number of other church people and to keep some kind of structure during this period.

(6) Groups are encouraged to be involved in outreach, care for the elderly, and other projects.

It became clear that if we wanted as many of our folk as possible in a group then we would need still more groups and would have to be much more aggressive about recruiting and training leaders for them.

In January 1982 we ran our own Bible study leaders' training course. This was initiated and launched by Tim Marshall, my curate. This multi-talented young pastor was also a gifted teacher and after the initial launch it was never too difficult to get people to attend. We asked the existing leaders to select potential leaders from their groups, and to this list we added the names of some who hadn't even attended a group regularly so far. We knew we had to be bold and trusting, and our attitude was wonderfully rewarded with very few problems. These people were invited to attend the training course and eventually most became leaders. The course has been run about two or three times a year, usually spread over two Saturday mornings from 10.30am to 12.30pm. Although the content of the course has developed since its initial launch, the outline is still basically as follows:

DAY ONE
Session 1   Small goups are important
   a) Church history and the New Testament show it.
   b) They meet our needs.

Session 2   Groups need leaders
   a) What is a group leader?
   b) What do I need to be a good leader? (Alternative leadership styles.)
   c) What a small group leader is ... and should not be.

Session 3   Groups are for fellowship
   a) How do we make our times of fellowship real and enriching?
   b) Helping the group to see its potential.
   c) Understanding the dynamics of the group.
   d) Understanding the most common needs an individual brings to the group.
   e) Effective communication.
   f) Adequate planning—different approaches.
   g) Problems of stagnation, difficult individuals etc.

Session 4   Groups are for praying together
   a) Reasons for praying together.
   b) Methods and ideas.

DAY TWO
Session 1   Groups are for caring
   a) The group in the pastoral context.
   b) Practical pastoral administration.
   c) Practical pastoral work.

Session 2   Groups are for study
   a) What are we aiming at when studying together?
   b) How to achieve these ideas.
   c) How to lead a study — basic tools.
   d) How to prepare to lead.
   e) What not to do.

In addition to the above, all suitable leaders now meet on three further occasions to discuss with my new colleague, Gary Rowlandson, the practical implications of becoming leaders. He has taken over the leadership and management of our Bible study network and its development now that Tim has moved on. In replacing Tim I looked for someone with proven administrative skills. Gary is very strong in this area and so makes light of much of this work. On these evenings Gary speaks to them further about leading and hosting their group as well as about choosing the most suitable evening to meet and how group leaders receive pastoral support in their work.

In addition to this we run in-service training sessions on the occasional Saturday morning, covering such subjects as counselling, pastoral care of the sick and the terminally ill, evangelism, and mobilising the laity. From all this it can be seen that we view leadership as critical to the growth of these groups.

The pastoral care of the leaders themselves and the group members is important. At the moment we have about thirty groups so it is impossible for the clergy to be intimately involved in all of them. We have had to add another tier of pastoral care between the clergy and the leaders of our Bible Study Fellowship Groups. We have formed three or four groups into a cluster group with a Cluster leader.

There are several benefits from this system, the first being in the realm of pastoral care. The leaders of the individual groups meet regularly together in their Cluster Group and share the needs and concerns of their own groups. The Cluster leader can offer support to the group leader and then, if necessary, pass on to Gary any issues he should know about. Another aspect of the Cluster system is that it provides an opportunity for the members of one group to broaden their circle of friends within the church. This is achieved by the Cluster regularly organising events for the groups within it. This might take the form of a social event, a meal, an outing, a picnic in the summer, or perhaps some kind of community action. Quite often such events have a spiritual theme and perhaps an outside speaker. In this way they provide an opportunity for worship and learning in a way that is often impracticable for an individual group. As these Cluster leaders meet with Gary regularly, and they in turn meet with their group leaders and hosts, a useful two-way channel of communication is provided. In addition to this I meet with all group leaders twice a year for encouragement, feed-back and information sharing. At these meetings we try to share problems, encouragements, ideas and various matters for prayer.

Then there is the pastoral care of the group members—about 300 people. Every church needs good structures to help it care properly for its people, the more so when it begins to grow quite large. We now have a membership of 582 and a regular Sunday attendance at worship of approximately 500 people. We have found our structure of home groups a great help in providing the pastoral support for our members that the clergy alone simply could not manage. They help considerably in making the church more personal and caring. I depend a great deal upon the information fed back to me through Gary's contact with the Cluster leaders and group leaders. Twice a year the group leaders complete a form giving details of the present membership of their group. This gives me and my colleagues on the staff team an idea of the movement in and out of the groups and alerts us to any specific situation that needs to be followed up. Leaders are expected and encouraged to make informal visits to their members from time to time.

As well as caring for the regular members of the groups we also need a system for integrating new members. Our concern is to integrate these newcomers into the family of the church as quickly and appropriately as possible.

Not all newcomers, of couse, are ready to join a Bible Study Fellowship Group immediately. In the pews of the church we have a simple yellow Welcome card. This asks for basic information such as name and address, and family details. It also asks whether the person is a visitor or not and how long he plans to be in the area. On the reverse there is an optional series of enquiries which many people complete. Alternatives can be ticked, such as 'I am not a Christian, but would like to find out more', 'I am a Christian and would like to become part of the church family'. About 150 of these cards are handed in each year which means we need a specific system for dealing with newcomers, just as we have for the Bible Study Fellowship Groups. We long to make sure that all newcomers to the church receive a warm and personal welcome and are followed up within the first few weeks of attending the church. In our system the home groups are responsible for 'fostering' newcomers. The system runs like this:

(1) On the Monday following completion of a card the newcomer is sent an invitation to a social evening which is held once a month. This enables newcomers to meet a few members of the church at one time.

(2) The following Sunday one of the Cluster leaders is given the name of the newcomer and is responsible for passing it on to one of the BSFGs who then seek to visit the newcomer and arrange to attend the same social evening as him.

(3) The BSFG then seeks to pray for its newcomer regularly, look out for him at the Sunday services, and if possible sit with him. They may invite him to any social activities run by their group.

(4) One of our congregation monitors the follow-up of those who fail to reply, or aren't able to attend an evening. He master-minds the whole system of invitations for newcomers and also arranges the evenings and tries to get to know as many as possible.

If the newcomer ceases coming to church or has other needs which the clergy should be aware of we are alerted to this early on. Each month the Cluster leaders ask their BSFG leaders and hosts to report on the newcomers they have fostered and appropriate details are passed on to the clergy at the Cluster Group leaders' meeting. Approximately three times a year my wife and I invite newcomers to an Open House at the vicarage which gives us an opportunity to meet them, and they us, in our own home. I usually say something about what the church has to offer, our main objectives and how we tick. I also say that in due course they will be invited to a lunch at the vicarage when we will explain our vision for the church and Christian stewardship.

I have become very aware that a number of folk come to us with no Christian background at all and without a real faith in Christ. So for several years now we have run a Starters' group which is a course of twelve sessions running three times a year. At the end of each course those who have attended are encouraged to become integrated into one of the weekly BSFGs. The Starters' course goes through the basics of the Christian faith as follows:

1 Getting to know each other.
2 The life of Christ—who is Jesus?
3 The claims of Christ—what he said about himself.
4 The death of Christ—why was it necessary?
5 The resurrection or Christ—did it happen?
6 The work of Christ—(1) sin and its consequences.
7 The work of Christ—(2) salvation from sin.
8 Making it personal—(1) discipleship, its costs and demands.
9 Making it personal—(2) The moment of decision.
10 Making it practical—(1) The Holy Spirit, prayer and Bible Study.
11 Making it practical—(2) Mission and evangelism.
12 A meal together.

Each person who attends is given an outline on the course and detailed notes each evening. We have found it best to produce our own materials for our Starters' course and our weekly BSFGs. These notes are written by members of the church, both clergy and laity, and then produced centrally. They are crucial to a worthwhile evening of study and sharing, and producing them is far from easy. In our experience the home-produced notes are appreciated more than those already published which never seem to meet our needs, aimed as they often are at very specific groups of people. Some groups have taken on projects period-ically, such as reading a chapter of a contemporary Christian book and discussing it over coffee at their meeting.

Although we already have about thirty Bible Study Fellowship Groups, we are always looking to form new groups. This is a painful but necessary business. People become attached to others in their group and don't want to leave, which is all very natural and good. But if more and more people are to benefit from Christian fellowship and Bible study, a price has to be paid. We do try, however, to be compassionate. By far the easiest way is simply to let a new group emerge. Someone offers to host a new group and we then find someone to lead it and a core of people to begin it. It is quite difficult to split a large group of fifteen or so people, but with care and tact they usually come to some form of agreement and a new group within the Cluster is formed.

I am very conscious that not all our members are in a group. We are therefore seeking to do all we can to increase the membership of groups, but we still need to make sure that everyone, whether in a group or not, has some kind of pastoral care. The church is the place above all else where people should feel loved and cared for. I would like to think that St James' is such a place. Although we often fail, we continue to set our sights high and endeavour to be a caring community.

6

Lay Leadership

Some folk are quite useless when it comes to practical things, but in my experience such people are often particularly gifted in other areas. I fall into the 'reasonably practical' category. I captained my school at both cricket and football, but as it was only a two-form entry that was no big deal! I have tried my hand at the odd conjuring trick, and even used one at a Christmas family service with some success. However, try as I might, I am no good at juggling. Attempting to keep lots of objects in motion in the air all at once takes a great deal of skill and practice.

I knew from the moment I became the ninth incumbent of St James' that somehow I would have to develop that kind of skill in terms of personnel management. There was a great deal to do and a new momentum needed to be created. Awareness of my shortcomings made me determined from the start to build a firm base of lay leadership as this was clearly critical to the life and growth of the church.

Developing this lay leadership was easier said than done. At St Matthew's, for a number of reasons, deci-

sion-making and leadership were largely by concensus.
It simply wasn't possible at St James' to discuss at the
level we had done for the last few years. I had to
become much more of an up-front leader, making
decisions and trying to take everyone with me until a
leadership team was formed that truly reflected the
new fellowship of St James' with St Matthew's. The
church I had inherited was very short of people who
had the leadership gifts to take us into the future. I
knew that I must not give the impression that the
amalgamation was really a take-over by the 'vicar's
people' who had come with me from St Matthew's. It
would have been easy simply to draw on the keen and
gifted leaders among them, but I was anxious that
they won for themselves the respect and support of the
St James' people. This was achieved quite quickly by
some, but others found this period rather painful and
difficult to cope with. I had to work very hard at
'juggling' as best I could, and I sought to build a staff
team as quickly as finances would allow.

I have found it necessary to develop this leadership
base with a mixture of paid and voluntary, full-time
and part-time staff. It seems that in places like Muswell
Hill, which is largely made up of professional and
managerial people who work long hours in demanding
and responsible jobs, the only way we can get their
commitment is to make sure we offer them the support
of administrative personnel just as they have in their
secular jobs. We certainly wouldn't have such high
calibre leaders involved with us if we hadn't been able
to develop this administrative base.

While our members appreciate the paid staff and
the clergy, I am sure that they would not feel it was
really their church if most of the leadership positions

were occupied by these people. Of course, the church expects certain tasks to be done by the clergy. But it is also happy for them to exercise a supportive role and give general oversight. It is so easy for the clergy to become involved in the detailed functioning of the church, leaving only very minor roles and activities for lay initiative and support. It is my experience that when jobs and even whole areas of work are delegated, they are usually, if not invariably, done better than if I had kept them to myself.

At first I was without any support except for three Readers, and even these I felt I couldn't overuse. At the beginning one of my main concerns was to implement the vision for Sunday worship as smoothly and clearly as possible. I may well have been wrong, but I refrained from putting these folk 'in the hot seat'. Paul Watson had been a Reader with me at St Matthew's. A very gifted person, I knew Paul wouldn't put preaching at the top of his list of gifts, so I held back on him, eager to direct him into other vital areas.

My other two Readers were from St James'. One of them was very elderly, quiet and frail, and the other, Norman Bellefontaine, was a much-respected member of the congregation who had taken the lion's share of the work for many years, including a great deal of preaching during the interregnum. During this time he also led the Children's Church every Sunday morning. In addition, he was one of the joint-treasurers and the leader of the only Bible Study Group I inherited. At the time of my arrival he was no longer a young man and was also supporting a sick wife whom he had married relatively recently. If anyone deserved a breather he did. I feel sure he did not approve of everything I did or how I did it, yet he was totally loyal and supportive. What was more he had the ear and respect of the long-standing members of St James'. I know that those early days were not easy for him as he was in a difficult go-between situation—a number of folk were turning to him to vent their feelings and reactions before tackling me.

On reflection, I suppose I wanted to give the impression that I could shoulder the work-load. My predecessor, Bill Allam, was highly respected and greatly loved. Although he had been a sick man for some time before his sad death, he managed to keep things together and coped valiantly. In the light of his example I felt I had to make my mark, and that meant doing many of the necessary jobs myself for a while. I off-loaded some of the tasks—mainly the 'back-room' jobs—but tried to keep the more public ones to myself initially. In those early days I felt rather like a one-man-band. I did, however, have some marvellous support and encouragement and was rarely impeded by anyone. Folk seemed to understand that I needed to get things sorted out before asking for their help, which was then mostly readily given.

Knowing that this situation could not continue for-ever, I was on the constant lookout for people who could quickly and effectively take up leadership positions. At this stage I also began to build a staff team both to support me and my work and to help give the pastoral back-up that lay leadership needs, especially in London. This latter point is crucial. In the suburbs of London such as Muswell Hill, as well as in the commuter belt, many people are keen to help but have limited time owing to their jobs which often mean they are not home until quite late. Weekends then become premium time for family and friendships, and evenings are exceedingly precious. It is quite tough on family relationships when the bread-winner doesn't come home until 7:00— 7:30 pm or later most evenings, and is then asked to attend a church function. But if the fellowship and ministry of the church is to deepen and grow, a firm and solid base of commitment is necessary.

We advocate membership of a Bible Study Fellowship Group for everyone. If you happen to be in a leadership position in some other aspect of the church's life this can all too often mean another evening out every week. By 8.00 pm, when most meetings tend to start, there has been space perhaps to help with bed or bath-time and reading a story. I have great sympathy when those who are parents of teenagers send apologies for absence from even quite critical meetings. While the younger childhood years are formative and shouldn't be neglected by caring parents, the teenage ones are definitely not the time to be away from home night after night. If ever there was a case for making a major withdrawal from outside activities and distractions, it is this. I have learnt that lesson the hard way.

For these reasons I have tried to keep a sizeable PCC and other committees so that no one feels under pressure to turn out when there is a crisis at home. I have always seen committees as supportive rather than critical. If the leadership is good it is not disastrous if a committee is poorly attended or even has to be cancelled. For some time now I have found our PCC most supportive. We have a total membership, including those who are ex-officio, of about thirty-seven. Although this is quite large, it means that our meetings are always held in a relaxed atmosphere and no one person is crucial to them. While I do my best to be present, I do not believe my absence would destroy the effectiveness of the meeting. However, I make a special effort to be present at the ones that are tabled, because absenting myself would give the impression that they are merely cosmetic—which they are not. We only hold committee meetings when they are necessary and we have something to discuss and decide upon.

At this early and formative period of the church's life I found it important when seeking leaders to choose people whom I could trust to get on with the job in hand without too much fuss and whose track-record was proven. Later I was able to be more relaxed about who should become leaders and I began to take bigger risks. I looked for people who could take decisions and lead from the front but who didn't feel threatened by others in their team or the church who had ideas on how their tasks should be accomplished. They needed to be able to learn from the insights of others: the perspectives of the people at St James' were often quite different from those of St Matthew's.

Thankfully, we have some very fine leaders who are willing to listen to one another openly and humbly. Indeed, I fear this is an area where the laity are often far better than the clergy. I like to think that I am quite adept at fielding difficult balls like awkward questions or suggestions that get bowled at just the wrong moment, such as at the church door as everyone is leaving after I have just given my all at one of the services. However, I recognise that I am not nearly as good in meetings, especially when a suggestion for improvement is made which seems to imply some personal shortcoming on my part. It is so easy to put people down and suggest they don't know the overall problem or even the facts. I fear this is an occupational hazard for clergy; laity seem not to be affected by it nearly so much. All members of a church constitute a holy and royal priesthood according to Peter, so they should never be made to feel less than that.

It is critical to have the right people in leadership positions and on the staff team—those who are truly called by God. Before I approach lay folk to ask them if they will consider accepting a position within the church, I usually consult others. I am then able to explain to potential leaders that they seem to us to be the right person for the particular task, and I ask them to view the appointment as a challenge and a calling, and to consider it seriously and prayerfully. I remember how encouraged I have been by the knowledge that I was called to my particular task, and I try to convey this to them. Despite this procedure, we still make mistakes by choosing the wrong people and neglecting the right ones.

When seeking leaders I always try to bear in mind that the membership of the church is ultimately God's doing. It is he who has given each of us particular gifts and talents for the enrichment of the church and its ministry. The challenge is to use the people provided by God. If they are submissive to Christ and empowered by the Holy Spirit such people are a powerful force. Indeed, it is our aim to mobilise the whole membership, but the constant flow of people joining and leaving makes this difficult. The population in the Muswell Hill area is quite fluid and this is obviously reflected in the life of the church.

One problem in looking for leaders is that often the jobs we have on offer seem so demanding. To fill them you have to be rather an exceptional person. But the church is no different from society at large, and such people are few and far between. Fortunately, we have some. However, church life cannot be held up while the search goes on for this rare breed.

The answer to this scarcity of 'big' people for 'big' jobs came to me while I was reading one of Drucker's interesting books on management. He illustrated a point he was making by explaining how industrialists and engineers solved the problem of a lack of skilled people during the Second World War. Apparently there was a very intricate component for an aeroplane engine that was extremely complicated to machine. The skill needed to manufacture this item was, of course, in short supply because many of the skilled men had been enlisted. The answer was to break the machining process down into nearly 200 small and simple steps, so simple that the unskilled labour brought in during the crisis was able to perform each small stage and achieve what seemed at the beginning to be one extremely complex task. This, surely, is the way most of us have to deal with a shortage of leaders. This shortage is often more apparent than real, for it has certainly been my experience that the moment small tasks are handed out you begin to discover people's hidden ability to take on greater responsibility. Thus what appears at first to be a shortage of leaders can often be resolved once people are willing to take on responsibilities, however small.

I have discovered over the years at St James' that it is important to make sure that there are always openings in the leadership team so that others can join. For those who are keen and gifted it must appear most unpromising to see the 'top jobs' apparently occupied for the foreseeable future. I inherited a system of two Churchwardens plus two deputy wardens. The latter seemed to be so only in name, not having any real tasks to fulfil. After eight years or so we now have two Churchwardens, eight Assistant Churchwardens, and four Deputies. All these are key people performing key tasks in the life of the church.

John Bailey, a valuation surveyor by profession, has been one of our Assistant Wardens for many years. For the past three years his specific task has been the fabric of the church buildings. He is extremely able, truly a God-send. While appreciating the importance of the buildings, he realises that 'they are not the real work'. He often says to me, 'If I do this, you and the others can do the real work of the church...' John has taken the burden of the buildings from both me and the two Churchwardens and we have made enormous progress in improving our fabric in a way we could never have easily managed without his skill and attention.

I have absolute confidence in him, which I feel sure he knows, yet he always sends me copies of the memos and letters he sends out. When decisions finally have to be made he sends me a note stating the options and the reasons why he considers a particular one to be the best. He usually encloses a letter all ready for me to sign. Very occasionally I will be aware of an angle on the matter in hand of which he might be ignorant, and we discuss this and possibly amend the letter or decide not to send it. Never once has he become irritated over any procrastination on my part, and even when my query has long since been anticipated and dealt with, he is courteous and gracious. If every church had a John Bailey it would be much stronger—its clergy less preoccupied with buildings and therefore the people better cared for.

Finding lay leaders has not always been so straight-

forward as this. I have been looking for lay leaders in
publicity and evangelism for several years now but
without success. We desperately need people to give
our individual efforts direction, cohesion and
encouragement. As we learn to do more without a
leader, it may be easier to find someone to take over
and move us forward. In my experience there is little
in church life that is static for very long.

The whole business of the recruitment of leadership
in the church is of critical importance. I dream of our
church growing in fellowship and effectiveness in this
area, of people being converted and growing in
maturity in Christ and going on to leadership positions
with the church. Indeed, it has been marvellous to see
young men and women grow and develop through the
life of the church, reaching positions of influence and
discovering potential and gifts they probably never
imagined existed in them a few years earlier. It is so
rewarding to see the pleasure and sense of fulfilment
on their faces after some ministry.

At the same time, I long for the majority of the
people to become shining stars in the dark night sky
just as the Apostle Paul longed for the Philippian
church—people who have applied their minds to
Scripture and also to their secular situation and are
seeking to shine with the light of Christ and the truth
of his Word in such a way that those around become
challenged by it and begin to turn to Christ.

My present Churchwardens are an illustration of a
dual development in lay leadership—one having been
a member of the church for some years, the other a
relative newcomer. Professor Harold Rodgers is now
in his eighties having had a very distinguished medical
career, latterly as Professor of Surgery at the University

of Belfast. When I arrived at St James' he and his wife, Margaret, had been attending the church for a few years. Both were mature Christians, yet Harold had never even been on the PCC, let alone anything more in the way of a leadership position. This oversight was not corrected immediately. Over the years I have discovered that it is often easy to pass over good leaders simply because they happen to have the supporting quality of humility. Harold was like this. He used to help with the gardening around the church and other menial tasks and he seemed to enjoy it. He was never pushing for a 'bigger job' and greater influence, and I was just as guilty of passing him by as my predecessors had been.

It wasn't until long after the two Churchwardens I inherited decided to retire that I discovered Harold. The previous two Churchwardens felt that the church would be best served if they made way for two new people, perhaps more able to help me and the church to move forward, though both had been helpful and played a creative part.

Brian Griffiths was a natural choice for one Church-warden, but when we came to examine our electoral roll looking for a second warden, Harold was once again bypassed. Instead we elected Paul Evans, a young man who had been part of the St Matthew's congregation. A year or so later I needed to replace him as he was going abroad, and it was then that I 'discovered' Harold. He had all the qualities one would wish for and more. What I realised then has been borne out by subsequent experience, for he has been in office ever since and played an enormous part in the developing life of the church. His graciousness and humility are a challenge to us all and he is a mine of ideas for helping the church and furthering its life. He is a fine example of what it means to be a loyal servant of the church and it is not surprising that he is now greatly respected as one of our key people. Most of us would describe him as a Christian giant—a larger than life person—yet he had been overlooked for so long. It is typical of his attitude that he has never once complained about this to me.

Harold and Brian served together for a number of exciting years. Brian has always been extremely busy and in great demand, yet this has never been a reason for him cutting back on his Christian commitment to his local church. However, when he was appointed Head of the Policy Unit at 'Number Ten' in 1985, after a good deal of heart-searching he told me he felt he could not do the office of Churchwarden justice and would have to retire. This was a sad day for me. Brian perhaps more than anyone else during this period had helped me personally. But the facts had to be faced and I am sure he was right. I know he has missed the challenge of the task and has found it frustrating not to be in the thick of things.

I now had to find a replacement for Brian, which brings me to the second point about dual development in lay leadership—those from outside joining us. Howard Cunnington moved into the area in 1980 when he joined the staff of our local Church of England comprehensive secondary school. He immediately made his home with us and quickly began to use his many gifts to good effect in the life of the church. Unlike Harold, he was a newcomer, he was young, and he was single—but these two together constitute a fine team. The Anglican system provides an excellent base for leadership and I have always tried to use it to its full extent. The Churchwardens are the duly elected bishop's officers and so fulfil a traditional but important role. They are elected by the vicar and people of the parish. They need to be a natural choice as far as the people are concerned, as well as being acceptable to the vicar. The position of Churchwarden is critical in any church. They are among the leading laymen in the church and so they need to have a real sense of tradition and yet a concern for the development of the church's life, ministry and membership. We have such in Harold and Howard. It is not surprising that I consult them frequently.

Much of the detailed running of the church for which the Churchwardens are traditionally responsible is now covered by our Assistant Wardens. This frees Harold and Howard to concentrate on the larger issues of church life rather than the detailed running of services and meetings Sunday by Sunday.

The Assistant Wardens are appointed by the PCC each year. In our case I have usually made suggestions to the PCC after having discussed the matter with one or two, and they have always approved my suggestions. At the moment there are two groups. In one group is just John Bailey with his responsibility for fabric. The second group consists of a number whose job is to lead and run a Sunday sidesmen team. They are responsible for manning the back of the church and making sure those tasks are performed which support the ministry of the church Sunday by Sunday. These tasks include: providing a warm welcome to all who come (especially watching for newcomers); showing people to a seat as and when necessary; collating orders of service and the notice sheets and giving them out; noting and recording attendance numbers; escorting the children to their activities part way through the service; taking the offering; ushering communicants, and tidying the church ready for the next service.

We have seven of these teams so between the Sunday mornings and the evenings they are only on duty about three times a year which means it is not an arduous task. In this way people can do this important work as well as having another job in the church which they might not otherwise have felt able to do if their turn came around too frequently.

Apart from Churchwardens and Assistant Wardens we also have four Deputy Wardens. Although each one has a particular area of concern in the life of the church which they are expected to monitor, their main responsibility is to support me and my ministry in the church and beyond. So for the first time since my appointment in 1978, I now have an official support group from within the church. At the moment this is still at an experimental level, but so far it seems to be working. For me this support group provides the fellowship that so many of the church members receive from the BSFGs. I am so glad to be able to meet with this group about once a month to share ideas and areas of concern. I do not of course divulge confidences, but I do try to be as open with them as I can. This support group consists of the two Churchwardens, the two joint treasurers, and the four Deputy Wardens. Attendance at this meeting is a high priority and so far we have had almost 100% attendance from everyone. However, it is of a size to make it possible for some to feel that they can, if necessary, be absent without the worry that they have spoilt the meeting.

As the church has grown and developed, I have tried to ensure that the leadership base keeps pace.

One book I have found most helpful is *Vision and Strategy for Church Growth* by Waldo J. Werning (Chicago, Il: Moody, 1977). Werning shows that in church we start off with a few leaders and the church a certain size. When the church begins to have a vision and to work it out in practice, the work develops so that the same number of people is endeavouring to cope with perhaps twice as much work. The church may continue to grow with the same leaders staggering under the burdens placed upon them, with the result that the additional work cannot be maintained for very long and is often achieved at some cost to the original membership and ministry.

The demands made on the team of leaders can often be too much to bear. The work increases for a time until the leadership problems begins to bite, then the team soon begins to diminish because individuals are unable to sustain the increasing demands being made upon them or are unwilling to sacrifice their family life and its responsibilities. The answer to this situation is perhaps obvious—to extend the leadership base as the church grows. I have tried to learn from this and make sure that as the work of the church increases and becomes more diverse, so we develop our leadership base to support it.

In quite a short time we have developed a sizeable lay leadership team. In addition to those already mentioned are folk who manage the various organisations within the life of the church, making the team up to about 120 people. Even so, this team is still too small for the current size and development of the church, so we are now eagerly looking out for more lay folk to help in this vital ministry. Some will be voluntary and part-time, others part-time but paid. This is in addition to our full-time paid staff. As the church grows, I am sure we will find that we have to keep increasing the number of those on the payroll.

7

Teamwork

As I have already shown, if a church is to have a strong
foundation to sustain it and provide a good base for its
ministry and growth, it needs a predominantly lay and
voluntary leadership. Sadly, when one asks folk whom
they think are the leaders in the church they often give
a list starting and even ending with the clergy. The
same idea is even prevalent among potential ordained
staff. They assume (though where they get this
assumption from I hate to think, surely not the theological colleges) that the moment they are ordained
and join the staff team in a parish, they have the
automatic right to be consulted and involved in church
decisions above many of the church members who
have been there for many years. I have always tried to
avoid staff meetings becoming a kind of 'upper house'
to the PCC. A new member of our ordained staff is
very much an 'assistant', even a 'junior', until he has
won credibility with the congregation. His reasons for
joining the church are very different from those of
other members and his commitment to stay is determined by factors which do not operate for others.
Fortunately we have had such a good selection of folk

on our staff team over the years that this has never been a major problem.

I have always understood my own role as vicar of a parish to be a unique one within the ministry of the church. A vicar is ordained by a bishop and accepted by a particular church as a pastor, to lead the people in work and worship. While this position is special, it does not imply leadership by just one person. I have always understood the other ordained staff as appointed to help me fulfil this calling. They are primarily assistants to me as the Vicar and not to the PCC. So they do not receive their directions from, and are not immediately accountable to, the PCC. They come, as I do, under the authority of the Bishop. Obviously this distinction very rarely raises its head, but I think it needs to be borne in mind by vicars and other ordained staff, as well as by PCCs.

Of course, if such ordained staff are people of calibre and spirituality, they will quickly win respect and trust for themselves in their own right and in quite a short time their views will be sought out and acted upon. This was certainly the case with my first curate at St James', Tim Marshall. Tim stayed with me from the time of his ordination in 1979 right through until 1985. As the years went by he became greatly respected and his opinions were sought for. I certainly saw him as a fellow minister rather than a junior. This he owed to the quality of his ministry and personal character rather than his position. I wasn't sure how things would hold together when he eventually had to leave for a parish of his own in 1985. Fortunately for us as a church and for me personally, the Lord, who is as always the Great Provider, has wonderfully filled the gap Tim left.

I have found the task of recruiting staff an extremely time-consuming and demanding one. I have learnt the hard way that it has to be done with great care as it can be very damaging to appoint the wrong people, for whatever reason, to a position. It can destroy the team spirit and nullify the value of staff meetings.

I usually take the initiative when looking for replacements on the staff team, but I do consult some of our key lay people for their views as to the kind of person I ought to be looking for and the skills and gifts he or she will need to bring. It seemed obvious to me that when I started seeking a replacement for Tim I would have to look for a man of maturity and calibre, someone in his thirties who had held an important position in the secular world before theological training. He would have to have almost immediate responsibility for some areas of our work and I knew I wouldn't have enough time to train a younger and less experienced recruit.

I had about a year's warning to find a replacement for Tim. It seemed a long time when I began the process, but the months quickly slipped by as I followed up various contacts. To each one I sent a profile of the life of the church and a broad job description. I followed up a number of leads and enquiries, all of which proved unfruitful. Men seemed very keen to come to us, but I had learnt to be careful. I knew that the kind of man who would continue and develop the work that had been begun during Tim's time with us would be hard to find.

Although largely in my hands, with the approval of the Bishop, I share the task of finding and appointing a new curate with a number of our key lay folk. I take a lot of trouble over this as I believe it to be a critical one.

I write the letters, sift the replies and have initial interviews with some, perhaps just taking them out for a meal rather than involving others at this stage. The process isn't taken any further unless I am happy with the person and his potential. If all seems well, I usually see the candidate a second time, hopefully with his wife if he is married. The next step is to ask him and his wife for a weekend with the church family. They usually stay with one of our key families and during the weekend visit several other homes with further folk 'dropping in' as well. In this way they are in fact interviewed and assessed. I brief all those involved, giving them notes and references about the candidate. They will also meet the other members of the staff team during this period and have one session at the vicarage to meet Mary, and the boys if they are around.

When replacing Tim, I still had no one very late in the year, and was feeling rather desperate to find the right man. I fixed an appointment to see David Wheaton, the Principal of Oak Hill College near us in North London. (A very fine pond in which to fish when seeking a curate, as I have discovered!) Fortunately for me, David remembered that Gary Rowlandson had just declined another parish and was now 'on the market'. When I met Gary I took an instant liking to him, and when I discovered what he had done with his life so far and followed up his references, it all seemed too good to be true. For several years he had been a secondary school teacher, rising to Head of Department for Religious Education. Just before going to Oak Hill for theological training, he held an administrative position at Hildenborough Hall in Kent and was much involved in planning evangelistic ventures around the country.

Gary has been with us now for two and a half years and it is great to have him around. Although his talents are different from Tim's, with strengths and weaknesses as with us all, he has become a close colleague and friend, someone whom I can trust implicitly. He is a great administrator and organiser. In his hands our Bible Study Fellowship Group network has been consolidated and developed. His wife, Diana, is now involved in helping to run one of our daytime Starters' groups along with another of our young wives.

The hard and sometimes rather tedious business of searching for the right person also applies to the position of deacon. In 1980 the Bishop rang and asked if I would be interested in having a deacon on our staff team. I met the person he had in mind but in the event she did not turn out to be the right one for us. But I continued to pursue the idea the Bishop had given me. Eventually, in 1983, Anne Hibbert was appointed as our deacon (or deaconess in those days). She was quite young but I and others thought that she would be a real asset on the staff team, bringing important complementary values. After the service at St Paul's when she was made deaconess by the Bishop of London, I commented to her that I had been ordained in this same place on the same date twenty years earlier. Her quick retort was, 'I was four!' I was old enough to be her father!

Anne brought great colour and many gifts to the church; she left us in 1986 in order to widen her experience in another parish. By then she had become well loved and appreciated by a good number of individuals, especially Tea Time members. Anne was very effective in her person-to-person ministry, and Tea Time grew out of a PCC discussion on how we could become more involved in the community of Muswell Hill, and it subsequently developed under Anne's enthusiastic leadership.

As a PCC we felt particular concern for the over-sixties. Tea Time is 'a place to meet and make friends'—and have tea. But what a tea! Each week the most splendid sandwiches are made by one of our members, Olive Hughes, and a rota of folk provide home-made cakes.

This tea is then beautifully laid out. From time to time a speaker is invited or some other event happens such as the banquets at Christmas and Whitsun. Anne did a great deal of the pioneering work in this area. Thankfully Caroline Thornton, the wife of our treasurer, has taken up the administration of the venture since Anne left us, and I am confident that Tea Time's ministry will grow and be a source of substantial blessing for the over-sixties in the days to come.

As important as the ordained staff are, I knew from the outset of my ministry at St James' that without lay support they would never be able to take us where I and others believed we ought to be going as a church.

The first lay appointment, as I have already mentioned, had to be a new organist. This appointment is always of critical importance, and I and many others readily acknowledge Alan's contribution to the growth of our worshipping community. Thankfully, there is now at least one agency whose main task is to help vicars looking for organists and vice versa. In Alan's case it happened to be a contact I followed up. The usual situation operated: someone knew someone who knew that Alan was ready for a move, it seemed he might be suitable for the task, and indeed he was.

Since coming to St James' I had received tremendous secretarial support from Mollie Ruscoe, who had helped my predecessor with some of his letters. However, this was only for one morning a week as Mollie had been retired for a number of years. The next lay member of staff clearly had to be a full-time secretary for me. When I put the idea to the PCC in 1979, the question was asked, as it has been on other occasions: 'What will she do?' When I had managed to convince them it would be a good idea, the further question came: 'Who will pay for her?' I had no idea who might rise to the challenge of working so closely with me and my administrative shortcomings, but I knew it would have to be someone with a missionary spirit! For we couldn't pay her the kind of wage she would rightly expect in secular employment, nor did we have an office or anything else to make it viable.

Providentially, the church had a real vision for this appointment. At the Gift Day on 21st July, 1979, it was agreed that to the normal appeal should be added the launch of an additional appeal to start a secretarial fund. A number of folk were sceptical as the Gift Day had rarely reached its normal target of about £2,000 over the past few years. What hope was there for a further £3,500 of which £3,000 was suggested for her initial salary? Fortunately this target was reached. Again after some searching, for I had a clear idea of whom I wanted for this position, Elizabeth Knight was appointed six months later with the official title of Parish Secretary and PA to the Vicar.

I had made it a deliberate policy to look outside the church for my secretary. I wanted to make sure there were no complications with this appointment. If she had been friendly with a particular circle of people within the church I am sure that others would have questioned how 'confidential' she really was. There has never been any such question raised about Elizabeth.

Elizabeth had trained to be a teacher of physical education and had held a number of teaching posts. She changed her career after a back injury and trained as a secretary. After some experience in a variety of jobs she spent two years working in Nepal with the United Mission to Nepal. Our paths crossed soon after she had completed a year at All Nations Christian College following her return from Asia.

Elizabeth began her work on a second table in my study, a very short-term arrangement as I needed my study to myself. Eventually we made my vestry in the church, just a few steps from the vicarage, into the parish office. Over the years I had learnt some lessons and read a number of books on management and administration, so I was now determined to get off to a good start and make the most of the marvellous opportunity of having an efficient person like Elizabeth on our staff team.

While I take overall responsibility for the administration of running the church, I try to delegate as much of the detailed work as possible. Although in practice Elizabeth looks after my diary and books meetings and interviews into the available time, I still try to keep control by planning my diary and indicating which time is available for what. Thankfully, because of her splendid eye for detail and concern to be as helpful as possible, we soon began a very productive partnership and with her support I am now able to deal with a very heavy workload and at the same time remain sane!

Initially she had to tackle a huge number of tasks. After several years, with the growth of the church and therefore of the workload involved in running the church, it was decided to appoint another administrative staff member. Much of Elizabeth's time had revolved around church matters, which meant that she tended to work on when most normal secretaries had gone home. (Indeed, this book would never have been written if this hadn't been sorted out!) This new appointment relieved Elizabeth of all those jobs that were directly related to the church rather than to me personally, thus enabling her to concentrate on being my PA.

I was glad when the Bible Society decided to move their head office from London to Swindon in 1985. Although it must have been very unsettling for many people, it did help to 'land' us Julie Goodwyn for this second post. She had been working for the Bible Society for a number of years and had decided not to move with them as her husband's job was in London. She had been a member of St James' for about eight years. As our church secretary, Julie keeps everything in control and is much respected by the church members. For a short while she also had the help of a part-time typist, as well as Mollie who still comes for half an hour a day each week though she is in her eighties. We are now actively looking for a full-time assistant secretary.

A further lay appointment to the staff team is Bill Goodman, our lay assistant. I first met Bill early in 1982 at one of our weekly Enquiry Times—an open time for anyone to come and chat or deal with matters such as marriage or baptism. Bill had been away at Gordonstoun School but was now back at home in

Muswell Hill. I had met him in church a few times. He was then terribly shy, so much so that he almost had a speech impediment. He could hardly string a sentence together and when he did so it took an age to get out! By that time I had usually guessed what he wanted to say anyway. On this particular visit he told me that he wanted to be a priest. I was rather surprised, but listened as he outlined his life so far. As he did so my initial reaction was of his unsuitability for the ordained ministry. Indeed, I wasn't even sure of his personal commitment to Christ! I spoke to him about the requirements for ordination and the kind of people likely to be accepted for training. I shared with him that I felt his first step should be to become a regular worshipper and get involved in the life of the church, joining one of our fellowship groups and perhaps even considering some other area of the church's life to which he could become committed. I left him to ponder these things and invited him to return to talk further if he wished. We prayed and he left. I remember praying for Bill that evening after he had gone home. I just couldn't see how he could ever become a priest.

Bill's life is a wonderful testimony to God's grace. He did get involved in the church and today, some five years later, I would certainly view him as a serious candidate for ordination training. When we began looking for some paid lay assistance for our youth work and additional book-keeping and computing assistance for the treasurer, Bill was an obvious choice. I asked him to consider the job, viewing it as preparation for further training as well as a kind of test for his future work for the Lord. Without his help, many important and widely differing parts of our ministry would be impoverished. He will turn his hand to any task, and although I am sure we have presumed upon his good nature, I have never heard him complain.

The latest addition to our full-time staff team is Michael Parker who joined us in 1986. Curates are in very short supply these days and to have two is a great privilege. When I was appointed Area Dean of West Haringey the Bishop agreed that I could have an additional curate to help me with my extra work.

It took some eighteen months before I found the man I wanted. This period was particularly busy and the reason for the delay wasn't simply the shortage of clergy who had already done one curacy and were looking for another. I wanted someone who would complement Gary's work and that of others on our staff team, as well as fitting in with us as a person. I also hoped that he would have the gifts to help us in the specific area of pastoral care. Michael met all these specifications. He and his wife, Jane, and their two girls joined us from Holy Trinity, Norwich, where he had served his first curacy. He is a very fine expositor with a pleasant manner and style. Michael also helps with our youth work which is in need of support and pastoral oversight. Both he and Jane have considerable experience in this field so I am very hopeful for some fruitful developments.

In addition to the full-time staff there are also some others. First to join us was Fergus Pearson, back in October 1981. Fergus has a degree in Fine Art and also writes poetry, some of which is published. Initially he was our caretaker and worked three days each week. He was concerned with all aspects of tidying, cleaning, maintaining and preparing the church and the church hall for services and activities. Working part time enabled him to spend the rest of his week pursuing his artistic interests. Fergus may well join the ordained ministry. Recently, along with several other lay members, he preached at one of our main Sunday services, giving a very fine exposition and clear presentation. I believe that he will be used by God in a wider ministry in years to come. In October 1987 Fergus became full time as a pastoral assistant to Gary. This new role provides him with an opportunity to prepare further for ordination.

Ruth Norman joined our church in 1979 when her husband, Peter, was appointed Head Teacher of our church school. About this time I was becoming concerned about our ministry to the children of the church. If our children's work was to develop in the way I hoped, we needed a new member of staff to help us. So, keeping to my general principle of looking to the church for personnel, I approached Ruth. The PCC were fully behind the idea and prepared for the cost involved. Ruth, a trained teacher herself, was appointed in September 1985 as our part-time children's worker.

Ruth has made a great impact upon this area of our ministry, giving encouragement and support to the leaders in our various departments from the crèche through Scramblers, Climbers and Explorers (the 0-11 years age range). She has achieved this by meeting with the different groups for planning and reviewing sessions as well as seeing them individually. She has also done a fair amount already to help develop the teaching methods and supporting materials.

In addition, various new ventures have been started or improved: a weekly Crèche Coffee, hosted by one of the mum's, at which mums and children can meet during the week, thus enabling the children to feel more secure in crèche on Sunday and happier to be left; the recruitment of people to welcome the children on Sundays; birthdays being remembered in the notice sheet and cards sent to the younger ones; the development of links between the family services and the work being done by the various groups so that, by rotation, the different age groups are involved in these services in some way; the development of our Toddlers' group with increased facilities, equipment and staff.

Ruth also does a good deal of family visiting, particularly those who are new to the church and have young children and those who have recently had their children baptised. She has developed a small team of visitors to help her in this huge task. There is no doubt that the children's work has developed and been enriched and in turn enriched the whole life of the church since Ruth's appointment. One of the most rewarding aspects of her work is the establishing of better links with church parents and the adult worshipping community. This is extended to the wider community as Ruth has ready access to our school as her husband is the Head Teacher. She has been quick to use the natural links with families that this provides, enabling us to make the most of the work being done in our school. I have never regretted making sure that I had a truly committed Christian as Head Teacher. Peter Norman has played a most valuable role in creating a school with Christian values.

More recently, Ruth has played a major role in launching our weekly Junior Praise—an opportunity for children in the under-ten group to worship in a way relevant to them. This takes place most Sunday mornings at 10.45 am, fifteen minutes before the main morning service begins. Ruth has done most of the spade work in launching this venture and, as well as

playing the piano for it, organises what we are going to
sing and chooses the team to help run it. I lead it
jointly with Jean Elliott, one of the teachers from our
church school. This is an exciting new development
with great potential for growth. It would not have
started without Ruth's involvement.

The staff team is a great bunch of people, but like
any team it needs to be managed and cared for. This is
my job, though everyone contributes towards the
team's well-being. I am still very much a learner in all
this, and thankfully they are all good humoured and
seem to cope remarkably well with my shortcomings.
They are all so gifted and committed that in fact I play
more of a monitoring role: encouraging them to develop
their areas of responsibility and use their time and gifts
to the best advantage of the church, helping to review
and suggest new ideas and developments, and sometimes giving fresh directions and objectives.

Vital to the health and direction of the staff team are
staff meetings. We have planned our staff meetings
with the aim of keeping a balance between meeting
together regularly and not leaving enough time for our
actual work. While wanting to keep in touch with one
another and our individual tasks, we are aware that
meeting too often can be fun but frustrating when it
doesn't leave enough working time. The best plan so
far is as follows:

(1) Every Monday: the full-time ordained staff meet
from 2-3 pm to review pastoral matters.

(2) Every Wednesday: the ordained staff meet from
8-10.45 am. This early start enables Paul Watson to
join us for part of the meeting before going to work.
The meeting is quite carefully structured with an

agenda prepared and if at all possible, circulated beforehand. Responsibility for the agenda is taken by each of us in turn thus ensuring that the matters that relate to our key areas of responsibility are reviewed regularly and developments and problems noted and discussed. My secretary Elizabeth attends this meeting to take notes and produce minutes with an action column. This action is reviewed at the next meeting.

(3) Once a month: all the staff meet, whether full- or part-time, on a Wednesday from 1-3.30 pm. Priority is given at this meeting to items raised by those on the staff who are not at the weekly meetings. Again an agenda is produced and minutes with an action column circulated by Elizabeth.

In addition to these meetings, all those who are able come together at 9 am each morning during the week for a short time of prayer and Bible study and on Wednesday for a snack lunch in the vestry. At a more informal level I try to meet each member of the full-time staff for lunch on a termly basis, occasionally we organise some social event for all the staff and their spouses.

Of all the areas of my ministry in which I have felt I needed most help, it is the one of staff management. I received no training at all at theological college in this area and very little since from the Church of England. I have had to rely upon my reading of some helpful books in this area and what I have picked up as I have gone along. I am sure the staff have suffered somewhat either from neglect or overwork and sometimes both, but they are very forgiving. I want to be a good team leader and I know I have to work at it.

We are very fortunate at St James' to have such a

number of full-time and part-time staff. This has been a deliberate policy. I have already indicated how important I believe it is to develop a leadership base as the work of the church increases. This leadership base is largely voluntary and lay, and it needs support and back-up as well as training. For this we have found it necessary to have full-time, trained staff. So far we have felt that our money is better spent on staff than the development of our buildings, though the latter hasn't been totally neglected.

Obviously, it is marvellous to have buildings that are ideally sited and well equipped to support the ministry of the church. However, I knew our financial resources could not possibly support such building works as well as the development of a paid, support staff team. I felt it was more important to mobilise the people of the church to the ministry for which they were called and gifted. So in the last nine years we have had no appeal or plan for any building project but have tried to follow through a rolling programme of improvement and development from our annual budget supported by our St Matthew's Fund, about which I will speak later.

The facts are that we have managed with our buildings and the church membership has steadily grown both in numbers and in type. But for our supporting staff team, we would not have been able to sustain this growth.

8

Money Matters

For most churches finance is a critical issue — no less
so for us. I inherited a church which, while having
some reserves, was nevertheless struggling to keep
abreast of its financial commitments. Its giving to
mission had been diminishing in real terms over several
years; the contribution to the Diocesan Fund was
proving more and more difficult to find; at the same
time the overheads of running a church plant the size
of St James' was becoming a burden for its congregation that was almost too large to bear. In 1975 the
contribution expected from St James' to the Diocesan
Common Fund was not paid in full. An even more
serious problem was that little had been spent on
bringing the various buildings and facilities up to date,
and there was no plan for continual refurbishment.
The financial backs were definitely towards the wall.

One of the benefits of the merger of St James' with
St Matthew's was that we were able to sell the site of St
Matthew's. It was about three quarters of an acre in
size. Out of the total realised from the sale we received

£81,000. As this was a capital sum it could not under church law be used to prop up our current account, but over the years it has enabled us to follow through a plan of capital expenditure to improve and develop our buildings. The game plan I inherited was 'survival' as with so many churches then, and the situation up and down the land has changed little since that time. Thank God ours has.

It was some time before I could concentrate on trying to change the financial situation I inherited in 1978, for other things took priority as I have already shown. I simply hoped and prayed that the giving to the work of God would improve until it was possible to have a more systematic and thorough overhaul of the situation. It took about two years for the scene to change. Unfortunately not enough to avoid a general atmosphere of caution when it came to looking at things we should be doing. I found this a real problem to handle at the time. I was very frustrated by people's apparent lack of vision and love for the church of Jesus Christ, and I felt ashamed at their seeming reluctance to be committed to what real church membership is all about. I was sure that a new and exciting kind of church life was just around the corner, but I had to be patient—these folk weren't misers, only cautious.

From the very outset of my ministry at St James' I often preached on the theme of The Church and tried to urge the membership, and especially the leadership, to consider seriously its privileges and responsibilities. Then in 1980 I began to speak to a few key people and the PCC about a thorough challenge to the church on the subject of Christian stewardship in all its aspects. I was eager that this should be done as a 'home-brew' venture rather than an imported plan from an outside body. I did not want to lose any opportunity to discover and develop our own leadership resources.

I knew that the choice of the leader of any such plan would be critical, as would be the membership of the action group needed to examine what was possible to achieve, and indeed the kind of programme needed to achieve it. The people involved had to win the confidence of the whole church, young and old, fringe and flock, the traditionalists as well as the more experimental and forward looking.

Those eventually chosen seemed to form very quickly into a well-balanced team earning the respect of the PCC and later the whole church. The programme was in practice quite hard hitting on a church that had not faced up to the issues of Christian stewardship in any serious way for some time. We decided from the outset to challenge the whole membership, which we considered to be more than just those on the electoral roll. We began to form a master list of those we felt would consider St James' to be their church. The smooth working of the action group, the efficient running of the programme that was thoughtfully and sensitively created, as well as the ultimate success of the venture as a whole, was largely due to the leader of the group, Richard Warren.

Richard seemed a natural choice, although I perhaps wouldn't have considered him a few years earlier when he couldn't have been described as one of our core members. Indeed, those who didn't know him well might have drawn the conclusion that he and his wife were quite nominal. They were neither members of a Bible Study Fellowship Group, not did they join in the prayer times and other similar activities which we had on occasions. Richard had been involved with the

Christian Union while at Cambridge University, but for various reasons had drifted spiritually during his bachelor days. Since his marriage to Karol, he had begun to return to regular worship. My predecessor, Bill Allam, had been a great help to them when they were married and the more I spoke to them both the more I believed in them. I had felt God guiding me to looking for *potential* leaders who would help forward the work of the church. At the same time I wanted to keep the rich diversity of the church intact and not make any of the different groupings feel excluded for any reason. Partly because he was not a core member at that time, on reflection I believe Richard to have been an inspired choice.

The planning group met to get things underway in October 1980. Although I was on this committee, I didn't always attend their meetings nor play a vital role when I did. Richard was in the chair and gave the impetus and direction to it all. I met with him quite often and we talked through possible ways forward, but my role in all this was supportive. These people were truly magnificent in their thoroughness and commitment. The aim of the group was to bring the church membership face to face with the challenge of Christian stewardship and hopefully to move us out of the hand-to-mouth attitude to finance and rather too frequent panic appeals to balance the books.

The programme followed our usual format starting with a meal and later making follow-up visits. The Diocesan Stewardship Office at Diocesan House gave us every encouragement and support. We began with a series of training evenings for those who would be making visits to those on the master list. We were concerned that those doing the visiting should be the first to respond to the personal challenge and also become effective instruments to share the challenge with the rest of the folk on our master list. This proved to be the case. The training programme was followed by two parish suppers, due to the numbers involved. They were both very exciting evenings and a fine example of delegation working at its best, Richard's team showing itself to be in a class of its own.

After the meal Richard spoke first, followed by me. He spoke so well that my task was almost done for me! People made a very positive response both by their words of encouragement on the evening, and more importantly in the way they rose to the challenge we gave them. The actual message about Christian stewardship was given primarily through a small brochure. The task of the visitors was simply as follow-up, to try to answer people's questions and to encourage them to make some response.

The actual programme got under way in late February 1981. Before then we had twenty-five covenants which brought in about £1,000 in recovered tax. The regular Sunday collections brought in a total amount for the year of about £13,000. Although by the end of 1981 we hadn't of course had the benefit of all the covenants that had been made that year, we did actually improve our situation as follows:

No. of covenantors: 155
Tax recoverable in full year: £9,000
Total gross income from covenants: £30,000 as compared with £3,000 in 1980.

This was most heartening for all of us. It was, I believe, a turning point in the life of the church.

The situation has changed even more radically since those days. In 1980 we had twenty-five covenantors and a total church income from all sources of £26,000 pa. Our situation at the end of 1986 was that we had 225 people covenanting to the work of the church and the total income in 1986 was £95,000, and £133,000 is anticipated for 1988.

A number of factors have contributed to this startling growth. First has been the leadership, inspiration and impetus given by Richard Warren and his team of leaders, visitors and helpers. It was natural for Richard to come to mind when those who had been joint treasurers for some time decided they ought to make way for others to take the church into its next phase. I didn't want to lose what had been achieved through Richard's leadership of the stewardship programme, so who better to look after church finance than Richard himself?

Unknown to me in the early days of our combined parishes, God in his wonderful way was preparing someone to take on Richard's mantle and the treasurership with a real talent for the task. Jonathan Thornton is the son of a clergyman, so he has a sensitivity to the demands on the vicarage as well as the pew. Prior to coming to us he too had drifted from his Christian roots while trying to carve out a career for himself in the City. After his marriage to Caroline he started to look again at the Christian faith through the marvellous ministry of All Soul's, Langham Place, that has been so helpful to many people over the years. His faith was reawakened and he attended their Core Year—a basic course in training for Christian service. During this time God was calling and preparing him to help re-establish a church which at the time he didn't even know existed. Jonathan has been God's gift to our church. Thankfully, God has given us others like him to fill important posts with real commitment, efficiency and grace by the power of his Spirit.

Jonathan and Richard were joint treasurers for a year before Jonathan took full responsibility as treasurer in May 1982. Under his leadership we have moved with some speed to build a much firmer financial base for our church's work. Our financial organisation is now a team operation. Some thirty-five people have been involved at any one time in the area of finance. Jonathan's team has consisted of:

— Collection counters: a rota of fifteen people.
— Stewardship visitors: a team of fifteen people.
— Income tax reclaim: administered by Bill Goodman using a purpose-made software programme.
— Cheque writing and basic book-keeping: Bill Goodman analysing all the payments and receipts in preparation for the computer bureau.
— Accounting: Joyce at the computer bureau processing the data and producing the financial accounts.

It is often the case that after a stewardship programme such as ours, there is a surge of interest in the church and giving to it. Frequently this initial enthusiasm soon begins to tail off. I was anxious that this should not happen at St James' for I felt that what we had achieved was really just a beginning and there was, and still is, a long way to go. So we developed a termly stewardship programme to keep up the impetus of the original programme. We aimed to draw in the newcomers to the church and also those who had declined to get involved in the previous programme but had now changed their minds. The Scriptures make it clear that there is personal blessing in giving and I was eager to introduce newcomers into this blessing as quickly as possible, both for their personal benefit and for the development of the church's ministry. Mary and I hosted these events in the vicarage. The programme included a follow-up visit in the same way as in the original programme. The figures below show how effective these have been:

	No. of new covenantors	Gross amount pledged
1982	23	£ 8,000
1983	28	£10,000
1984	26	£12,000
1985	21	£ 7,000
1986	33	£12,000
1987	38	£13,000

A glance at the above table shows that we had problems in 1985, perhaps our most difficult year since 1980. We were experiencing continuing growth in the congregation Sunday by Sunday, but a number of internal pressures were distracting us from the important task of incorporating newcomers into real membership both in financial terms and in terms of involvement in the whole mission of the church. The finances were still growing. At this time we were trying to improve the quality of our pastoral support and administrative base, and so we made the bold decision to employ another secretary to look after the administrative affairs and give greater back-up to the pastoral staff, leaving Elizabeth freer to help me with my growing commitments.

I was by now quite heavily involved in teaching church growth principles for the Bible Society's courses. In January 1985 I was made Area Dean of West Haringey which added more responsibilities to my increasingly busy timetable. In addition Tim, who had now been with me for some six years, was ready to move on and was beginning to look for new pastures. This inevitably meant I had to spend a good deal of time and energy searching for a replacement for him and also for a new second curate. It was also at this time that a number of our key leaders in the church changed jobs and found themselves, for a little time at least, unable to give me and the church their usual level of support and understanding. Finally, we had to find a replacement for our organist, Alan, who was also on the move.

While our inner core was continuing to develop its vision for the church and was committed to it both in time and finance, we failed to keep the growing need for practical and financial support before the whole congregation. As a consequence, the needs of the church were not met. Most of the congregation considered the church a 'rich' one, forgetting the greater vision we had for it. We have never seen our task as building reserves, but rather using money to implement our vision of what God wants to do with us and through us.

Another contributory factor to this situation was that in 1985 all those covenants that had been made in 1981 came to an end. The sum involved was £30,000 which was given by 155 people! We knew that to avoid losing this, people had to be encouraged to renew their covenants. Efforts were made to deal with the matter—no small task. A considerable amount of paperwork and administrative hours were spent on the project. Naturally, there were some cancellations of covenants for domestic reasons and moves to other parts of the country. But incredibly that figure of £30,000 was actually increased to £35,000 as people not only renewed but increased their giving. Again, much of this work was done by Jonathan Thornton but now with the backing of Bill Goodman and the office in general.

Yet another problem we faced was the diminishing team of visitors who originally trained in our programme in 1981. At the end of 1985 we made a feeble attempt to halt the slide. This lacked the usual back-up and planning, and we used a number of untrained visitors who in some cases, because of their lack of training, actually put people off commitment rather than encouraging it. We learnt our lesson and asked Chris Gillman to lead a major communication offensive with the church membership. With newly-trained visitors and specially prepared Bible studies for our home groups, we sought to remind people of the vision and their duty. Thanks again to Jonathan Thornton and also to Chris, who proved to be God's man for this task, £23,000 was pledged from this venture, reflected in the figures for 1987.

Another major factor in the continuing growth of the church's finances over the years has been the staff fund. Originally this was the secretarial fund initiated in 1979 to pay my secretary's salary. I soon saw that if we were to grow and develop we would need additional lay staff for whom, of course, we would have to pay. I talked it over with Jonathan and suggested launching a fund to support an increase in our lay staff team. People could contribute units of support, each unit being £50 pa. I spoke to the PCC about the work in the church that needed consolidating and developing, as well as the work that we needed to initiate. Thankfully, this idea was enthusiastically taken up and the staff fund was launched in 1983 and has grown steadly:

1979	–	£ 3,900 (secretarial fund)
1980	–	£ 1,800
1981	–	£ 4,700
1982	–	£ 6,000
1983	–	£13,000 (launch of staff fund)
1984	–	£23,000
1985	–	£28,000
1986	–	£35,000
1987	–	£38,000

(These figures for the staff fund are included in the total income for the Church mentioned previously.)

In fact, but for this fund, we would have been in serious trouble in many ways, not least in the task of recouping tax from the growing numbers of covenants. This is because a good deal of the administration involved in this exercise is done by Bill Goodman, our lay assistant, who is of course supported by the staff fund. In the early days it took six people about six Saturday evenings dealing with the paper work for the Inland Revenue. In 1984 we installed our own computer to help us with this and other projects, and most of the work is now done by Bill. Over the years the 'tax man' has made a growing contribution to the life of our church for which we are extremely grateful.

Year	Tax Recovered from Covenants
1980	£1,000
1981	£3,000
1982	£6,000
1983	£10,000
1984	£14,000
1985	£18,000
1986	£18,000
1987	£21,000

Through the support of Bill and our finance team now numbering about thirty-five volunteers, we have been able to increase the list of regular givers while at the same time absorbing the losses that happen to all churches in areas such as ours where the population is always changing. This effort has produced, over the years, a quite dramatic change in our financial situation, from an income of £19,000 in 1978 to £111,000 in 1987. For all this we praise God and rejoice that through the work of his Spirit so many of our folk have found the grace to be truly committed, and this is reflected in their generous giving.

Thankfully, our giving to the support of mission has seen a dramatic increase over the years. This is a very exciting development, one that is capable of further growth.

Donations to Missions

1978	£ 1,400
1980	£ 3,500
1982	£ 8,000
1984	£13,500
1986	£15,000
1987	£15,000

As a Church we are not complacent about our finances, and we do not think we have reached our peak. Despite some major efforts over the years, a high percentage of our income still comes from a very small percentage of the congregation. This is not because we have a few who are very wealthy in comparison with the rest, nor because we have many who are poor. We do have a fair number of elderly and retired folk and a few students, but most people are salaried. Yet so many of them have not yet discovered the blessing of allowing the Spirit of God to enable them to 'give liberally'. Exciting therefore as the story of our financial development is, it would be even more remarkable if all gave as they could. We would then be able to tackle a great deal more for God, both in Muswell Hill and beyond.

If finance is a critical issue for the church then surely the administrative burden that clergy have to bear is similarly critical. Young clergy are often put into situations that are very depressed, as I was both at St Matthew's and St James'. They may have few administrative skills and little experience and training to help them deal efficiently with the work load that faces them, let alone the skills required to help lead the church out of depression and plan for future development. The problem is compounded if there is very little lay support because of the sad state of affairs in the life of the church. The whole business of seeing what needs to be done and sorting things into priorities is not easy when the entire work force, except for the clergyman himself, is working on a voluntary basis. It is not unusual for clergy to discover that they cannot find a lay person who is able and willing to take on the role of PCC secretary with all that is involved in minute-taking, typing and producing copies for the meetings. Similarly on the financial front, many churches are in serious trouble simply because their treasurer has been below par. This is due either to a lack of skilled people in the church, or because skilled people are just not willing or encouraged to get involved.

How are we to get people involved in the life of the church? How are we to motivate them, once they do volunteer, to reach high standards of performance and effectiveness? How are we to communicate with this group of people about progress, or indeed problems and how to avoid them? These questions can be daunting to the most experienced. But how would some of our top business executives fare if their only workforce was voluntary?

The key to getting members involved and committed to the work of the church is giving them a vision of what could be achieved with God's help. At the same time they need to be shown something of the privilege of being called to be involved, and encouraged to have a sense of duty that will move them to be more committed. One can readily see that the tasks awaiting a new incumbent moving into a depressed situation quickly begin to multiply. Add to all this a lofty vision for church life that will be far more demanding upon clergy time, which is pressed already, and you have the ingredients for church decline, or at best a plateau situation, and clergy breakdown. All too often clergy are trying to cope in such a situation, while people expect them to spend every day visiting the faithful, be at church meetings every evening, and on top of that be full of spiritual vigour on Sunday.

Although I had some experience of management

and administration in industry, those who knew me as a curate would not have described me as particularly efficient or well organised. It was not until I became Vicar of St Matthew's that I realised to what extent I had failed to develop and use the skills and abilities which I had acquired in my industrial experience. In my first year at St Matthew's I made a number of resolutions, one of which was to endeavour to be efficient during my ministry there. Sadly, that aspiration was not achieved. When I eventually came to St James' and was able to employ, in due course, a secretary, I was absolutely horrified at the thought of what she would discover—piles of unfiled papers and unanswered letters—certainly not signs of efficiency.

Many a church has floundered through lack of financial resources and insufficient administrative support and aid. I am very glad that I saw the need to do what I could to make sure that these were our strong areas rather than our weak ones.

9

Mobilising the Flock

Ever since my first Sunday here at St James', as I have
said many times, the expectation that I and others had
was that we should not just become a lively church but
an influential one. This vision could not be realised by
the leadership and staff alone, however good they
might be. Along with plans to develop the leadership
and staff base of the church, as well as the worship,
fellowship and finance, was a vision to mobilise the
membership and develop an understanding of mission.
Of all our plans, I knew this would probably prove the
most difficult one to implement.

A number of St James' members were loyal supporters of missionary endeavour overseas, but at St
Matthew's this aspect of our life was greatly under-
developed. Nearer home, both congregations knew
about their evangelistic reponsibilities, but neither
had seen a great deal of fruit in this area, nor was it at
the top of their agendas, though for quite different
reasons.

At St Matthew's we had tried to reach out to the
neighbourhood with one-off and special activities as

well as more prolonged drives. This took a considerable effort as there were only a few of us and the community around seemed especially unresponsive, as it had been for many years. If our motivation for evangelism wasn't great, it was due to constant disappointment. It seemed as if we had tried most things, but had largely failed. But everyone viewed the 'church on the hill' as a place of great opportunity.

As a church we have much to be grateful for. We have a prime site on the top of Muswell Hill—opposite Sainsbury's and the main shopping area. Unlike St Matthew's, which was tucked away off the main thoroughfare, we are on several main bus routes and at the geographical heart of a thriving community. But I knew that this prominent and central position wasn't enough on its own. We couldn't simply open the doors and expect people to come in. Despite the enthusiastic efforts of individual members, whose light burned brightly and who longed to see more life, the church had actually been in decline over a number of years like many in England today. Built at first as a small church, it was rebuilt in 1910 to hold more than 700 people instead of 250. Despite the current gloomy situation, many of its members still considered that St James' should be a large and influential church in the neighbourhood and the wider area of North London.

I knew it would not be easy to turn a pattern of decline into one of growth, but I knew this was what God wanted so I never for a moment thought it would be impossible. This was due, I believe, not to any extraordinary amount of faith on my part but the support and encouragement of a number of folk in the church. Brian Griffiths was there at first behind the scenes, and then as Churchwarden. Harold Rodgers

joined him later to form a marvellous duo of help and
support. Although from time to time we had to engage
in heavy discussion over some problem, my lasting
memory of this period was of Brian's special ability to
make one feel larger than life. What he expected to be
achieved often staggered me, yet it wasn't long before
I believed that the expectations were possible and
actually began to work towards their realisation.
Harold, as always, was willing to do anything to help
and would ever add a word of encouragement. However, in those early days I knew that before these
expectations could ever be realised I would have to
embark on a major reshaping of my own ministry and
make a serious attempt to bring as many of the church
members into active service as possible.

In the old days at St Matthew's I was, because I had
to be, a jack-of-all-trades. Whatever needed to be done
I usually had to organise and also be the main labour
force. Our finances were never strong enough for us to
employ contractors for repairs, so it was always DIY.
Not that I minded at the time, it was good, I thought,
to show I didn't consider myself above such things.
However, I couldn't contemplate working in this way
at St James'. Thankfully the main church building
was in good order, but that couldn't be said for the
church hall or the vicarage. Fortunately the Diocese
had put in hand a very expensive plan to update the
vicarage and improve it for us. It is easy to be wise
after the event, but I sometimes wonder if I was right
to tackle so much by myself in the past. To some extent
it may have been at St Matthew's, but some aspects of
my ministry, particularly in the realm of pastoral care,
certainly suffered and there was some disquiet about
this. I found this very hard to handle at the time as

most of the folk were single and those who were married didn't have children—certainly not four boys as I had, two of whom were teenagers. This tough period could be described as the seven lean years. Mary often found things almost impossible, but soldiered on.

I vowed I wouldn't make St James' a repeat performance, but I knew things wouldn't be easy. Before we took on the job I told Mary that the initial two years would probably be the most difficult, and so they proved to be. I promised her I would make every effort to keep our 'day off' sacrosanct during this time, and I did, and have since to a large degree. I did warn her that I would have to put a lot of time and effort into these first two years. This meant that for the first year, because I was working from the study in St James' vicarage and we were still living at St Matthew's, I was gone from the house for a large part of the day. It was a tough time for Mary and the boys, but I am not sure that it could have been avoided.

I knew I had to do all in my power to avoid becoming too heavily involved in the detailed running of the church, but always try to stay one step removed thus making sure I could monitor what was going on and what more needed to be done.

In the days at St Matthew's, practically everything we did was discussed at great length. The inner core of the church would meet often and talk into the early hours of the morning. It wasn't very unusual for the PCC meetings to go on until 11 pm and after. Consensus was the style. I am sure it was right to work like that at that time, but it was tedious and wearing. I knew I couldn't operate like that in the new situation. For the first year we still had two PCCs until the legalities caught up with us and we were officially gazetted as a joint parish. I then had to rethink how I would operate and what my priorities would be.

I knew I would have to be more businesslike in everything I did. I longed to be an expert church builder like the Apostle Paul. The doctrine of the church became a major theological interest of mine, leading to an ever-deepening love for the church of Jesus Christ. I wanted to keep time for preparation and reading, for I knew I would have a large preaching load initially. I needed time to plan for the growth of the church. In addition, I knew I would have to put people as a priority. I planned my diary as best as I could to keep these things in line.

The aim of trying to mobilise the church into action again was bound to be difficult and could be thwarted by a number of things. There was then and still is to some extent quite a large number of people connected with the life of the church who are fairly nominal in their commitment to Christ. At the time some of the church members thought I would achieve nothing until this nominality problem was dealt with. While I was in some agreement with this, I couldn't adopt their solution of getting rid of the nominal Christians somehow, which led some to suggest that I was compromising the Gospel. We had a large list of people with whom we were in contact, and my goal was not to weed out the believers from the nominal but to win them all. I wanted to see a work of grace take place in all hearts, whether they resided in the nominal or active part of the church or at stages in between. Obviously, if the church remained or became even more nominal then that would be serious. It is clear Christ isn't pleased with Christians who are such in name only (see Revelation 2 and 3). I did not believe, however, that a head-on confrontation with the church over this issue was appropriate; they would not have understood the issue. I felt then, as I still do, that what would win these folk wasn't all-out war but love. So I preached Christ and called for people to respond to his call for discipleship, for people to follow him in active obedience to his word and example. It is significant that some of our most active members today would have been described as nominal in those days.

Unfortunately, some did feel that they couldn't stay. Thankfully there was not an exodus, simply the odd one or two here and there. Indeed, some have actually returned to us. It saddened me to see people leave, for I felt I had failed them. Had they really understood the message of Christ or was it that they simply couldn't cope with the way I presented it? I suspect there was much of the latter.

During the early years when I tried to awaken this body of Christians to their responsibilities, I really tried hard to win the ones we had. It is easy to wait for keen Christians to come in and help get the show on the road, but I tried to avoid that. I often preached on the nature of the church and what it should be doing in the world. Slowly but surely our giant started to come to life. The people of Muswell Hill began to take notice and to come and see what was going on. Wasn't this how the early church made its mark on the pagan world in which it lived? As Michael Green observes in *Evangelism in the Early Church* (Highland : Crowborough, 1984): 'their community life, though far from perfect, as Christian writers were constantly complaining, was nevertheless sufficiently different and impressive to attract notice, to invite curiosity and inspire discipleship.'

I believe that it is because the church today is so different from the early years that few people take it seriously. Generally speaking, the church doesn't seem to turn people to Christ, but sadly the very opposite. Robert Powell, the actor who played the part of Jesus in *Jesus of Nazareth*, said 'I didn't believe in Christ before I began this part. But I do now; what I have read and experienced and played has had a profound effect upon me.' However, he went on to say—and here is the challenge and indictment—'I have not been converted to the church but I have been convinced of the divinity of the Man.'

The scandal is, as Michael Green has pointed out, that people like the Christian message, they listen to it, and think seriously about responding to it. But they cannot take the church; they look at us and are turned off. Why? Largely because we are so nominal—Christian in name only. This is certainly the case in the areas in which I have gained my pastoral experience—*among evangelical Christians*. There are many evangelical, nominal Christians and if all of them came to life there would be a revival.

Over the years it has been my great joy and privilege to see people of all ages come to enjoy life in Christ. Very few of them have easy or straightforward lives, yet they have exhibited a special bearing which is clearly from God.

In the last two years we have seen six of our men accepted for theological training prior to ordination. All of these have a special story to tell of God's grace and goodness as well as his equipping for service. In the last two years two of our young women have responded to God's call to serve him overseas. Let me tell you about one of them, Margaret Howarth, an attractive young lady in her twenties.

Margaret joined us having moved to London to look for a job as a librarian for which she had just qualified. She had been brought up in a Christian home, and her parents were missionaries in France for a number of years. She was very shy and quiet but didn't strike one as a person with real problems. However, I was soon to realise this was a myth.

Margaret had a long history of depression and had for years battled against the thought of being inadequate and inferior. But, through the help of Christian friends she met in our church, and others, she gradually gained a bearing that she had not known for some time. We all began to admire her tenacity and grace. She has been on medication now for some years and has often expressed a wish to be free of it. So far this hasn't been possible, but this hasn't held her back.

Remarkably, in spite of her history, Margaret was eventually accepted for short-term missionary work. She has now completed it—and with full colours. She once wrote to me, speaking of her series of depressions and breakdowns:

> I can see how God has 'restored the years that the locusts have eaten'. I am a very sensitive person by nature and always wanting to help others. I realise that my natural qualities can by used by God and all the hard experiences have taught me that God is sovereign, that he uses difficulties, even health problems, to mould us into the people he wants us to be. For a very long time I feared the trials that God would put me through and I was very fearful of reaching another breaking point. But as I have meditated on Scripture and looked closely into why God allows trials, I really know that I can trust God with the future, whatever it brings.

Through the experiences, God has made me into a whole person. I now have normal relations with Christians and non-Christians alike. I enjoy meeting new people and feel free to be myself with most people. Occasionally I have to battle with the the old inferiority complex, but now I can deal with this myself.

Sharing intimately with a few select people has also helped me to come to terms with my personality problems. Whenever I feel tension I go to someone I can talk to—sometimes it has to be God and me. Through the years I have come to accept that God is healing me every day. The mere fact of taking my injections regularly means that I keep well. I have come to see them as my regular 'vitamin' supply. God sometimes chooses medicine to heal; we don't always see a supernatural healing. If I were to try to wean myself off the medication, medically speaking I would be endangering my health. Having lived with the consequences of not taking medication I would be foolish to try to do without it.

My stability, I believe, lies in the fact that God has given me a medication which my body needs and functions well with. I also attribute my mental stability to a renewed relationship with God. It took years before I could talk to God just as I would to a friend. I know I owe my remedies to the prayers of many people, both friends of the family and my own friends.

Also I look at my bad days, and I accept them with the good days. Life, I have discovered, even as a Christian, is not all on one level. Many things can cause us to have blue days but it's great to know that Jesus stands with us in those darker times. Jeremiah 29:11 has become a real promise just for me: 'I know the plans I have for you', declares the Lord, 'plans to prosper you and not to harm you, plans to give you hope and a future'.

We are exceedingly proud of Margaret.
Then there is Dr Catherine Griffiths. She and her

husband, Max, who is also a doctor, joined us after many years of membership at All Souls, Langham Place. Their only son, James, joined our Cub and Scout groups because they lived in Muswell Hill. At that time they started to attend our monthly Family Service and then eventually joined us on a regular basis after much encouragement from John Stott and other members of the staff at All Souls. I began to become acquainted with the family and discovered that Max had never been confirmed. It was a joy to be involved with them over this and I began to get to know them better. It has been wonderful to see them both grow and develop as Christian people, especially over the last few years.

When Catherine was diagnosed as having advanced metastatic cancer there was little the medical profession felt they could do except try to keep the disease under control until a cure was found—or there was some other miraculous intervention to deliver her from this terrible disease. Catherine responded to a letter in the *Sunday Telegraph* on 27th July 1986, writing of her treatment by chemotherapy: 'Patients on chemotherapy certainly require much support and encouragement and this I have received abundantly from family, friends, colleagues, doctors and nurses, but more especially from the prayers of fellow Christians, known and unknown, and I feel that God has most definitely had a hand and a purpose in my response to date.' I had the great privilege of being involved in a service of healing for her at which we prayed for her and anointed her in accordance with Scripture and the Prayer Book.

Catherine was a most remarkable lady. I saw her at her worst moments when death faced her head on.

Through these moments and the better ones, I was profoundly amazed at her grace and fighting spirit, coupled with a genuine and most attractive humility.

Her actual death was quite a remarkable experience for those of us around her. It came very suddenly in the end. Max was able to get her into hospital and was a model of devotion and care. I spent several hours with her towards the end. For a good deal of this time she alternated between consciousness and unconsciousness. While conscious one of the things she often wanted was a drink of cold water. Unfortunately, because of her serious condition, this could not be allowed to settle in her stomach for any time or she would vomit, so I took my turn with Max at aspirating her stomach with a Ryle's tube. The other thing that she frequently wanted in her lucid moments was for me to read 'her' Psalm. This was Psalm 23 which has been a source of help and strength to many. I read from her Bible and I couldn't help but notice every time I read it that the last verse was heavily underlined: 'I know that your goodness and love will be with me all my life and your house will be my home as long as I live.' I remember that after reading she exclaimed with a twinkle in her eye 'That's my insurance!' I am sure I shall be better able to face my own eventual death and cope with any personal trauma that might come my way having known Catherine Griffiths.

It has been marvellous to see the church expressing its renewed life in vital worship as well as in the corporate life of fellowship and caring. However, a church as physically prominent as ours, presiding over Muswell Hill in all its regal splendour, could not but be expected to have an influence on the community and church beyond Muswell Hill and its immediate surroundings. In a small way that ministry has already begun, and much sooner than I expected. This influence has spread in a number of ways and to differing areas of the church.

Muswell Hill comprises a sizeable group of people who are only resident for a short period of time. St James' partly reflects this aspect of the population. A good number of our members, who have seen the need for a church fully committed to worship and fellowship as well as mission, have been scattered to many different places in this country and abroad. As I have already mentioned, a number of these have actually begun training for ordination to the Anglican ministry. One of our talented young men became the Archbishop's research assistant and is now the Diocesan Secretary of the Liverpool diocese. Others, having moved away from the area, have quickly become involved in their new church. Here they often help to set up Bible study groups and for this purpose, they may well ask for sets of our Bible study notes and Starters' course to help them get under way. Over the years I have received a number of invitations to lead courses connected with church growth that were initiated by such people.

Through my chapter in *Ten Growing Churches* (Bromley: Marc Europe, 1984) and my connection with the Bible Society's church growth programme, I have been involved in leading a fair number of courses up and down the country. Sometimes these have been mixed denominational groups of people but often individual Anglican churches, as well as clergy conferences and local clergy meetings. I have travelled to Norway and Belgium to conduct similar courses. It is interesting that the invitations are given not so much because of my talent and ability, but simply as a result of what people have heard is happening, by God's grace, in the life of the church here at St James'. More recently we have begun to receive invitations from churches to which other members of our staff have been able to respond. These enquiries have been about such matters as setting up Bible study groups and working with computers.

In the Autumn of 1987 we launched our first major evangelistic programme which we hope will be on-going. Using our natural network of relationships and contacts within both the church and the community, we set up a team under my colleague Gary Rowland-son's supervision to launch this venture of faith and enterprise. The idea was to use the talent and experience of some folk from St Helen's church, Bishopsgate, to run a number of dialogue suppers. The speakers at the suppers were members of the team from St Helen's. The idea was that during this venture not only would people be reached for Christ but our own folk would be trained and gain experience so that we could run similar programmes each year and at the same time begin to think about helping other churches with their evangelistic outreach. This has already begun to happen.

In the whole area of mission, however, by far the most significant influence is the impact individual members are having in their place of work and among their friends and neighbours.

I shall conclude this chapter by coming full circle to the place at which this book began, and tell of the grace and bearing of another remarkable lady, Elizabeth Blakelock, the wife of the PC killed in the Tottenham riots. Many were impressed by her interview broadcast soon after Keith's death, and guessed correctly that she was a Christian. Through the witness of the church, and especially our Deacon, she had become a committed Christian just a few months before the tragic and brutal death of her husband. Her faith has been sorely tested. She would readily admit she has had bad days, yet to us she has been an outstanding example of what it means to be a Christian in adversity.

The church is the family of God. It is an enormous privilege to be a part of that family here at St James'. This family will, I trust and pray, grow and develop, both the individuals within it and corporately, to be more and more what God wants it to be—a light that 'gives light to everyone', the 'church on the hill'.

10

Conclusion

The past few years at St James' have been exciting and exhilarating as we have seen the church grow and develop. In this chapter I will seek to draw out several of the factors which have contributed to that growth and development.

Awareness of the importance of the church

As a new Christian, worshipping at St Mary's, Ealing, I quickly began to appreciate the ministry and fellowship of that church. Later, through my reading of Scripture I began to understand God's purpose and plan for his people, the church. Ever since those days I have been keen to broaden this understanding.

I was excited then, as I still am, when I considered God's great missionary plan to draw to himself a community, from all the nations of the world, to enjoy his special presence and be a part of this great divine scheme. I never cease to be inspired by the vision first received by Abraham so many years ago that God had a plan to bless 'all peoples on earth' (Gen 12:3). The great plan is still on course, but since Christ it has taken a new turn as Paul outlines in Ephesians 1-3. Now the church is included in his loving desire to bless 'all peoples'. Clearly, this blessing comes primarily 'through Christ' and is to be enjoyed 'in him'. Because of who he is, God did not have to involve anyone in bringing about his purposes, nevertheless he has chosen to use us. This is a great privilege and responsibility.

The title of David Watson's book *I Believe in the Church* (London: Hodder and Stoughton, 1982) poses the question, who believes in the church? Sadly, too few. Thankfully, an increasing number of people at St James', some of whom have been Christians for many years, have come to believe in the importance of the church in their own spiritual development and that of their family and friends, as well as the community of Muswell Hill and beyond. They believe that the church is precious to God and so to them. As a result they worship regularly and give freely of their resources and much of their spare time in the service of Christ. This awareness is not as widespread and as total in our fellowship as I would like it to be, but it is there and is a major factor in our development and growth.

To some extent this understanding has been due to a frequent focusing on the church in our teaching and preaching. But above all it has come about by spiritual experience. Folk have known and seen and started to understand what it really means to be part of the household of God, the church.

The centrality of worship

As I have already indicated, I tried to plan and lead the Sunday services so that they would become an effective vehicle for our praise and adoration of God and a central part of our new life as a church. I wanted the services to be clearly God-centred, enriching for the congregation and therefore attractive. At the time I did not realise the importance of this desire and plan and how elusive it was to be in its realisation. For all the shortcomings of our Sundays, they have contributed to the growth of the church as we have sought to make all who come feel at home and involved.

The sense of mission

From my first day as Vicar of St James' I have had a deep sense that what was being done in closing one church and joining another, as well as beginning a new ministry, was not merely for the benefit of the present members of these two churches alone, but for the mission of Christ in the community as a whole. It is, of course, always important for the present members of the church to understand that they are loved and valued. Yet it is also important that this sense of mission—this living for others—should permeate the whole life of the church.

The newcomer and the visitor have always been important to us. We quickly found that we had to develop a proper structure to make sure we were doing all we could to help the stranger feel part of the church family as soon as possible. Sadly, I am sure there are people whom we have not welcomed into the life of the church as we ought. Nevertheless, this sense of mission has been another contributory factor in our developing life. In addition to this concern to welcome and nurture those who come into our church, we have longed for some years to have a regular evangelistic programme that would develop and become part of each year's activities, a programme to reach not only those who come in, but also those who do not. Such a plan is just beginning to take shape as I have shown in chapter 9.

The regular fellowship

I learned the importance of fellowship during my days at St Matthew's, discovering just how much could be achieved through regular times together. This was especially so through our weekly Sunday lunches. From the outset at St James' I knew that I had to do all I could not just to bring two congregations together into one, but to create a new fellowship out of the two. This was, and still is, vital to our church life. There is now a tremendous amount of valuable Christian ministry going on week by week in our Bible Study Fellowship Groups—work that could not be achieved through the Sunday services alone. The church has developed this network of family cells which has greatly contributed to what has already been achieved. I talked with Eddie Gibbs who was at the time working with the Bible Society. I shared with him my concern for wanting to keep the sense of family in the life of St James' and to develop it as we grew in numbers. Eddie suggested that I visit some of the large churches in California and spend some time studying with Peter Wagner at Fuller Theological Seminary. I was able to do this during some sabbatical study leave. While in America my conviction about the strategic importance

of these small groups was confirmed and it has deepened over the years.

The need for adequate staff

Some people will perhaps be surprised (though not all
I fear) when I say that by temperament I am basically
lazy. That is why I am so good at relaxing! My major
problem is getting going and keeping at it. Thankfully,
by the grace of God I'm highly motivated in the service
of Christ and the work of the ministry. I knew at the
commencement of my ministry at St James' that if I
was to reach any of my goals and achieve what I
believed God was looking for, then I would need
support and help.

I am grateful that, from the begining, the Bishop
promised a curate, but I knew even in those early days
that this vision for the church would need not just one
additional colleague but a team of full and part-time
workers. Over the years I have worked at this, putting
it as a high priority financially, and placing it above
building needs for a number of years. The salaried
staff situation is very different to what it was in 1978
when I became vicar. I am sure that we would not
have achieved as much as we have, from the human
standpoint, without the help of our staff team.

The emphasis in our staffing policy has been twofold.
First to add to our team those who could help us with
pastoral work. I have always felt that in the church we
should aim at giving quality care. In this area we are, I
believe, still rather understaffed. But for the present
pastoral staff's hard work, the situation would be more
noticeably deficient than it is.

Secondly was the need for support in administation.

Although I have some ability in this area, I knew I couldn't possibly manage without a lot of help. While I had to take responsibility for the smooth functioning of the church, the task of planning, organising, staffing and co-ordinating couldn't be done single-handedly if the church was to develop as I hoped it would. Those on our staff team who help in this way played a major role in the whole of our life and growth. Today, after nearly ten years at St James', I am more than ever convinced of the need for an adequate staff team. So often churches try to develop and grow around one person. That is not the case here. The base of our ministry is much broader and the steady expansion of this ministerial base has contributed to our renewal.

The deployment of the members

The mobilisation of the people of God is of critical importance. We have always tried to help everyone who worships with us on Sundays to be involved in the work of the church in some way. In ten years we cannot, alas, announce total success, try as we might. But the concern to help people discover their gifts and use them in and through the life of the church has been a most important ingredient in our corporate life. This has been a demanding task with the number of jobs ever increasing as the congregation has grown and the church's programme and work has broadened. It hasn't been made any easier by the highly mobile population of our particular parish in London.

An inspiring vision

My wife Mary often reminds me of that touch of Walter Mitty in me. I am sure she is right, and my sons will confirm it. However, my dreams for the church here are not of that order at all. I have always felt deeply that God wanted great things for St James'. Regularly sharing this vision for the church has contributed to its vitality. Each year, different aspects of our life have come to the forefront of our attention. While most of us greatly value the life we enjoy here now, it is the future that occupies most of our attention, for without that forward look we would stagnate. I am not the only dreamer of dreams in Muswell Hill. Many of our members share my passion for the church. It is not unusual for one of them to come and see me and share a vision for their particular area of concern, as indeed do the staff team. Not only have I had encouragement in this dreaming from the Christian community here at St James', but also at a wider level and in particular from the present Bishop of Edmonton, Brian Masters. Without his support for us as a church and his encouragement to me personally, a great deal of our growth would not have happened. Sadly, many of us clergy are so individualistic that we want to go our own way, but I have found enormous strength from those set over me in the life of the church. We have been most fortunate in our area of London in having bishops with a great compassion and concern for the church of Jesus Christ.

Gavin Reid, in his introduction to *The Crisis Facing England's Church* writes:·

The Church of England, viewed in numerical terms, is a minority group within a minority group. What is more, it is a minority group that is still shrinking in numbers to the tune of 1% per annum.

Such chronic decline has a basic effect on morale. I sense that underlying almost every official report and developed strategy coming from the Church of England, there is a resignation to the inevitability of decline.

In the postscript to the same book he writes:

Hope for the Church of England rests with the parish churches and I've seen enough of them to be optimistic. It is true that many of our parishes show little evidence of new life or growth, but an ever-increasing number have exciting stories to tell and can see where they are going. Probably twenty per cent of our churches are growing numerically and I would guess another thirty per cent have stopped shrinking.

I, too, am optimistic about the Church of England. I hope and pray that this story of one parish church may help to create more optimism among others.

The British Church Growth Association

The British Chruch Growth Association is a co
ordinating body for those interested in the growth
(spiritual, numerical, organic and incarnational) of
the British Church today. It comprises researchers,
teachers, consultants and practitioners who share
information, insights, experience and a new thinking
through regional and national activities, a regular
journal, occasional publications and other resources,
seminars and conferences. It is based at St Mark's
Chambers, Kennington Park Road, London SE11
4PW.